10649702

Bad Press

Bad Press

The Worst Critical Reviews Ever!

Laura Ward

BARRON'S

First edition for the United States and Canada published by
Barron's Educational Series, Inc., 2002

Produced by PRC Publishing Ltd.,
8–10 Blenheim Court, Brewery Road, London N7 9NY

A member of **Chrysalis** Books plc

All inquiries should be addressed to:
Barron's Educational Series, Inc.
250 Wireless Boulevard
Hauppauge, NY 11788
http://www.barronseduc.com

International Standard Book No. 0-7641-5539-3

Library of Congress Catalog Card No. 2002107112

Printed in China

9 8 7 6 5 4 3 2 1

Contents

Introduction

"If you can't say something nice, don't say anything at all."

Shakespeare? Whitman? Huckleberry Finn? No, a rabbit called Thumper, courtesy of Disney cartoons. If we all followed that advice, though… well, most of the writers represented in this book would have been nursing ulcers from imploded rage. After all, it's better to let it out than to keep it in—or so they say. To swallow Thumper's homily the gene for malicious glee would first have to be removed. There's something in all of us that enjoys the cut and thrust of a good verbal joust. And it must ever have been so. For as long as the public has listened to, watched, read, sat through, or endured the musical, theatrical, or literary fruits—or other less high minded endeavors—of creative minds over the centuries, there have been individuals ready to pipe up and voice their own opinions on the subject in hand.

After all, some plebeian in ancient Athens must have found Homer's epics too long, or a merchant in 17th-century Amsterdam of the mind that twenty years' navel-gazing on the part of Descartes for the nugget, "I think, therefore I am," frankly, a bit rich. Surely there must have been one medieval squire who did not subscribe to the complicated business of courtly love as bandied about by the troubadours? And wished that Lancelot and Guinevere would just, somehow, get it together.

It goes without saying that not all of these Joe Publics put pen to paper to voice their grumblings. And writing reviews—literary or otherwise—must from the outset have been a minority interest. Yet few can have had a desire to "correct" as grandiose as that attributed to Alfonso X "the Wise," 12th-century king of Castile and Léon: "Had I been present at the Creation, I would have given some useful hints for the better ordering of the universe." Nonetheless, we can only agree.

Call it what you will: voicing an opinion, offering one's two cents' worth, reviewing—and how much more civilized that sounds—or, put bluntly, criticizing: all stem from the same root—the pleasure of nit picking, dissecting, altering, and basically "improving" upon what is already there.

Yet at its most basic level, the reviewer's task is a matter of giving a straightforward commentary— taking, say, a book, play, or movie, and giving an outline of the plot, characters, and setting, along with a clue as to the dénouement. Then, at the end of it all, providing an even-handed account. "Buy it," "go see it," "read it," "try it," may be the kindly verdicts. This is hearty fodder for the intellect and soul—an incitement to self-improvement, even.

Secretly, though, our baser nature delights in the other, less worthy approach. One can imagine, for example, that a theater-going Londoner in Elizabethan times would have been edified, but perhaps a trifle disappointed, to hear only that "Master Shakespeare writes excellent plays." More scintillating to discover that Richard Burbage, the leading actor—failing to convince as Cleopatra—had fluffed his lines, slipped off the stage, or had stinking vegetables flung at him by a baying crowd. There's a thrill to be had in reading the painful dissection of a literary reputation, the lampooning of a new Broadway production, or thumbs-down on a pretentious restaurant or dumb television show.

And there's the rub—one sure-fire reason for our enjoyment is our own inarticulateness; we just aren't up to the job ourselves, so secretly admire those who have the nerve to broadcast from the rooftops what we only dare to mumble. There may be other, more ferocious, reasons for our enjoyment lurking in the murky depths of our psyche—a taste for verbal warfare as ingrained as the urge to trounce another, to gain the upper hand.

However, anyone can call a spade a spade—it's the fact of doing so with wit, flair, and verbal virtuosity that marks out the sharper minds from the rest. The most memorably excoriating reviews stay in the mind not just because they are "mighty mean," but because of the turn of phrase or *mot juste* that makes for the perfect put-down ("I wish I'd said that!").

The English have long had a reputation for this, in the "arsenic and lace" vein (or rather, iron fist in a velvet glove). Oscar Wilde was—and still is—seen as the great genuis of this technique, even applying it to himself—for instance, of one of his own plays that had flopped, he is reported to have said, "The play was a great success, but the audience was a disaster." Dr. Johnson before him turned out one-liners by the yard—"Your manuscript is both good and original; but the part that is good is not original, and the part that is original is not good."

However, the Americans have shown that they can beat others hands down on this—witness Dorothy Parker, queen of the barbed response, with "This is not a novel to be tossed aside lightly. It should be thrown with great force." Or, Mark Twain (Samuel L. Clemens) with the splendid put-down, "A very good library could be started by leaving Jane Austen out." This is the technique at its best—a sentence that passes almost unnoticed, but which, immediately after, brings the reader up short—and gives the greatest glee.

Alternatively, and battling fair to be the most succinct theater review of all time, there is the one-word notice "No:" a newspaper critic's economical response to a London show with the "asking-for-it" title *A Good Time.* Or, on a more (or less) musical note, Ethel Merman's no-nonsense take on Cole Porter: "He sang like a hinge." (No one could accuse her of beating about the bush.)

Another critical technique is the "rant," which gives rise to merriment not only because of the quantity of bile contained within it, but also because of the total lack of inhibition. Gabriel Harvey displayed a particularly creative flair for this type of invective when he wrote of the 16th-century English playwright Thomas Nashe:

"… vain nashe, railing Nashe, cracking Nashe, bibbing Nashe, swaddish nashe… roguish nashe… the swish-swash of the press, the bum of impudency, the shambles of beastliness… the toadstool of the realm."

The writers of yore do seem to have been particularly good at letting it all "hang out," no holds barred —even the polite-sounding *Literary Gazette* commented of Walt Whitman, "Of all the writers we have perused, Walt Whitman is the most silly, the most blasphemous and the most disgusting." Disgust seems to have been the contemporary response to many of the 19th century poets, including John Keats ("piss-a-bed poetry") and Percy Bysshe Shelley ("a lewd vegetarian"). Personal it certainly was. Disgust did not die an early death, though—in fact, "Absolutely disgusting" was the first movie review. The author of *Lady Chatterley's Lover* could find things pretty revolting, too: D. H. Lawrence of James Joyce's *Ulysses* wrote, "The last part of it is the dirtiest, most indecent, most obscene thing ever written."

In an earlier time, the French writer Claude de Saumaise's preferred treatment for the English poet John Milton (author of the epic "Paradise Lost") was "to hang him from the highest gallows, and set his head on the Tower of London." Which is nothing if not final. Perhaps the writers of yesteryear had more time in which to hone their instruments of torture, and a climate of attack and verbal insult in which to thrive—who knows what they would make of our "modern" genres of cinema and television.

The modern twist is sophistication and irony—and it became an art form with the members of the "Round Table" group at the Algonquin Hotel in New York in the 1930s. The group included such rapier wits as Alexander Woollcott, Robert Benchley (whose shortest theater review is reputed to have been the comment "Dun't esk"), Walter Kerr, and, of course, Dorothy Parker. Needless to say, the art is still very much alive, and kicking. Witness Gore Vidal, of his fellow countryman Truman Capote: "Truman Capote has made lying an art. A minor art."

Which just goes to show that the bitterest attacks are often "inside jobs"—onslaughts by fellow writers and artists, rather than by the professional critic. Mark Twain put it another way: "It takes your enemy and your friend, working together, to hurt you to the heart; the one to slander you and the other to get the news to you." Yet nothing quite matches in tone Beethoven's verdict of the composer Rossini— "Rossini would have been a great composer if his teacher had spanked him enough on his backside."

Some of the most satisfying reviews are those that ripped to shred works which, in the intervening years (centuries even), have become classics—those volumes of which Mark Twain said "everybody wants to have read and nobody wants to read." Even Shakespeare was not without his detractors. Samuel Pepys, the diarist, found him tedious; George Bernard Shaw loathed the bard. In the *Saturday Review*, May 1897, Shaw wrote: "*Antony and Cleopatra* is an attempt at a serious drama. To say that there is plenty of bogus characterisations in it… is merely to say that it is by Shakespeare." Yet George Bernard Shaw suffered from poor reviews himself ("the exuberant, infertile figure of G.B.S.," was Kenneth Tynan's verdict).

Then there's always the off-the-cuff or off-the-record remark, the reported speech that becomes legend. The phrase "Guido Nazdo was nadzo guido" —the verdict on an actor with Latin good looks but small talent—has been attributed to both George S. Kaufman and Brooks Atkinson. The composer Sir Thomas Beecham was renowned for his caustic remarks ("It's like a lot of yaks jumping about," he remarked of Beethoven's Seventh Symphony).

As much as anything, the publication in which a review or critique appears will influence its approach. An article in the "red-top" press is not going to take the same angle as a piece in, say, the *Wall Street Journal*; while a write-up of the new opera at the Met will be in a different tone from that of the latest CD by Limp Bizkit. Or, indeed, the reporting of the newest food fad on the West Coast. Space is an issue—some truly hilarious accounts need room to breathe, for the story of the terrible event to unfold. Food criticism is a case in point— the scene is set, and even has its characters in the shape of waiters and dining room managers. When you read food critic Dara Moscowitz's opening gambit, "There I was, withered to my bones with dehydration," you know things can only get worse.

Whether expletive or expounding, all the reviews in this book have been chosen because they come down firmly on one side of the fence—they never sit on it. Boos, catcalls, and badinage; all aspects of criticism are represented, and by no means exhaustively. This is just the tip of the iceberg, and the selection is necessarily subjective. Critics and reviewers are often attacked as the "stupid who discuss the wise"—but sometimes the work under review is neither witty, nor wise. And deserves its drubbing? That's for the reader to decide.

Laura Ward
March, 2002

Movies

I like a film to have a beginning, a middle and an end, but not necessarily in that order.

Jean Luc Godard (attrib.)

Smut—and there is no other name for the thing the pictures have been retailing—is no part of any kind of art or even pseudo-art…

How the intelligence of a public is to be affronted and how its cultural rights are to be invalidated by eliminating from the movies scenes in which Mr. James Cagney pinches his old grandmother on the bottom, literary moments in which Mr. William Powell, surprised by an intruder while he and a lady are seated respectively on a water-closet and a bidet, jocundly observes, "That's all right; we're only chatting," and episodes in which Miss Mae West sardonically employs her spacious backside in lieu of repartee, I should like the anti-censorship crusaders… to explain to me.

George Jean Nathan

By science fiction standards, a mortal virus is the cheapest of gimmicks, since it requires nothing more expensive than a lot of people who can lie down.

Kenneth Tynan on *The Satan Bug*

Produced by ageing French enfant terrible Luc Besson, *Kiss of the Dragon* is a slick, international mishmash that takes place over 48 hours in a Paris where everyone speaks English. [...] This witless, almost plotless picture is a succession of noisy, violent shoot-outs —in a four-star hotel, a couple of restaurants, an orphanage, an underpass, on a Bateau Mouche—and the body count both of cops and innocent bystanders would keep Paris's *pompes funèbres* and gravediggers working day and night for a week. Burt Kwouk is on hand as Li's loyal Parisian contact and his puzzled look suggests that he expects his old boss, Inspector Clouseau, to appear and take over the case.

Philip French on *Kiss of the Dragon*
in the *Observer*, 11 November 2001

The basic feel of *Carmen* is "What's the use?" Godard can hardly bring himself to throw up his hands. He gives the impression that maybe he'd rather sit around listening to Beethoven's late quartets than make movies.

Pauline Kael on Jean-Luc Godard's *Carmen* in
The New Yorker, 17 September 1984

After three parts of *Back to the Future*, innumerable (and clever) time-warp *Star Trek* adventures, and decades of *Quantum Leap*, time travel as a subject is rather ho-hum. (Even Jean Claude van Damme has done it.) I can't believe that kids will emerge from *The Time Machine* saying anything other than, "Those Morlocks kicked ass!" Nineteenth century readers—and impressionable 20th century adolescents—had their minds opened by Wells; in the new millennium, his great-grandson [Simon Wells] has made their world a little smaller.

> **David Edelstein** in *Slate* on *The Time Machine*,
> directed by Simon Wells, 8 March 2002

A slapdash, poorly acted, paint-by-numbers teen horror comedy, the sequel is too frenetically edited to build any suspense, and its special effects are strictly bargain basement.

> **Stephen Holden** on *An American Werewolf in Paris* (directed by
> Anthony Waller) in *The New York Times* on 25 December 1997

At least it manages to be an equal-opportunities offender by characterising all Brits as stuffy, pompous and bumbling and all Yanks as violent, avaricious and philistine.

> **Kim Newman** on *The Mummy* in *Sight and Sound*, July 1999

If I was the ghost of Marilyn Monroe and had a few good friends high up in the councils of the Society for Psychical Research, I think I might sue for defamation of ectoplasm.

> **Benny Green** on *Goodbye, Norma Jean* in *Punch*, October 1976

Re-prehensible, re-heated, and certainly not re-commended.

> **Jack Yeovil** on *Repossessed* in
> *Empire magazine*, issue 18, December 1990

This sleek, Cliffs Notes version of a masterpiece is so glossy and picture perfect on the surface and hollow at the core that it might be described more accurately as Ralph Lauren's *Anna Karenina*. Not a hair is out of place or a dust ball visible in this 1990's travel-poster vision of 1880's Russia as the vacation paradise of your dreams. […]

The movie's biggest mistake is the casting of the French actress Sophie Marceau (Braveheart) in the title role… Ms Marceau's most ardent expression is a fixed, unsmiling stare with the corners of the mouth turned down.

Stephen Holden on *Anna Karenina*
in *The New York Times* on 4 April 1997

Makes you long for something lighter and wittier such as a documentary on the Khmer Rouge.

Simon Rose on *Shanghai Surprise*, 1986

There is a smiling, gracious staleness about *The Yellow Rolls-Royce* that gives it the air of some long-forgotten ceremonial occasion —the investiture of Dornford Yates, perhaps, as a Knight of the Garter. The stately blandness of its manner is quite at odds with the fusty triviality of what it has to offer: it condescends from a great depth.

Kenneth Tynan on *The Yellow Rolls-Royce*, directed by
Anthony Asquith from a screenplay by Terence Rattigan

The most compelling thing about them [Streep and De Niro] is the beauty-spot wart on De Niro's cheekbone: it has three dimensions —one more than anything else in the movie.

> **Pauline Kael** on *Falling in Love* in *The New Yorker*, Dec. 1984

Overall, I would say that this is an ape film that has gone to the dogs.

> **Steven J. Willett** of *Rant n Rave* (www.rantrave.com)
> on *Planet of the Apes*

Ms. Lee's makeup is painted on so heavily that she may not even be able to change expression. On the other hand, there's not much about *Barb Wire* to make her want to...

She is described by production notes as "a woman with high standards in a world of lowest common denominators." Not about to raise those denominators one jot, Barb lurches through a trashy, violent action film that will appeal only to comic readers, curiosity seekers and prison inmates throughout the land.

> **Janet Maslin** on *Barb Wire*, which starred
> Pamela Anderson Lee, in *The New York Times* on 3 May 1996

If I had to think of one nice thing to say about this movie it would be... the next movie that I see (I don't care what it would be) would be a hell of a lot better. In the opening credits, we find out that this movie is based on an idea by the Spice Girls and Kim Fuller. This was probably the funniest moment, because just knowing that it took five Spice girls and one normal Kim to split an idea amongst themselves and come up with this schlock I found to be amusing.

Steven J. Willett of *Rant n Rave* (www.rantrave.com) on *Spiceworld*, the Spice Girls' movie

An experience so vacuous it's almost frightening…

Ian Birch on *Xanadu*, which starred Olivia Newton John, in *Time Out* magazine, 1983

To sit through this film is something like holding an elephant on your lap for two hours and fifteen minutes.

Time on *Circus World*

[It] not only neuters its characters, but, failing to achieve the pathos the genre demands, sells off its birthright for a mess of kitty litter.

Leslie Felperin Sharman on *Tom and Jerry: The Movie* in *Sight and Sound*, August 1993

And it's jolly japes a go-go time as Dave (he's fat ergo he's funny) Albinizi (Coltrane) is mistakenly elected as Pope! What will the portly innocent do when he discovers that The Vatican finances are being filched and squandered by his sparkly-robed officials? And how will he cope with the heavily signposted news that his glamorous ex-girlfriend (D'Angelo) has had his son (Getty), and he's a pop star, and he's got a frightening Cockney accent (dubbed), and he's on his death bed... and that the very same baddie who put him there wants our chunky chum out of the way too? Most importantly, can Peter Richardson's fumbling hand find the button marked "comedy" before the end credits roll?

Well, no, he can't. Limp writing, leaden directing and a series of toe-curlingly-unfunny "situations" sap the energies of the almost-famous comedy cast until not even Herbert Lom can wring a laugh from the damp script.

Miranda Sawyer on *The Pope Must Die*,
with Robbie Coltrane and Beverly D'Angelo,
in *Empire magazine*, issue 26, August 1991

Mister Moses is the one about the African village that must either quit its ancestral home to accommodate the new dam or stay and get drowned. Like most films, it stars Carroll Baker. The running time is 115 minutes; the walking-out time is much earlier. The weather throughout is excellent.

Kenneth Tynan on *Mister Moses*.

Richard E. Grant, though equally stranded by the script, is a cut above, but his presence... simply serves to remind one of *Withnail and I*, making one wish he'd whip out his wellies and a couple of bottles of vintage claret and start tormenting the villagers. It might have made things more bearable.

Demetrios Matheou on *Food of Love* in
Sight and Sound, November 1999

In it, a lot of people (and a helicopter) are eaten by a shark, and a great deal of incompetence is shown by all. Among those asked to behave like village idiots are Roy Scheider, Lorraine Gray, and Murray Hamilton. Script is by Rentascream. It's odd that the good people of Amity, Conn. should take so little notice of the evidence of a shark lurking off the shore of their little seaside resort. Surely someone in the cast must have seen *Jaws*?

Barry Took on *Jaws 2* in *Punch*, January 1979

Eyeing the muscular Ben as he toils at the oar, Quintus Arrius (Jack Hawkins) is plainly boiling with suppressed lust. Is Quint a queer quaestor? Perhaps he is a poofter praetor, soon to become a camp consul. "Hail Jupider!" cries Stephen Boyd, who is either playing a particularly bad Roman or else playing a Roman particularly badly. Rather than stick around for any more of this, Jesus takes the easy way out.

Clive James on a Christmas screening of *Ben-Hur*, in the *Observer*, 30 December 1979

In fact the paradigm for the action in these recent Woody Allen movies is high school. The characters in *Manhattan* and *Annie Hall* and *Interiors* are, with one exception, presented as adults, as sentient men and women in the most productive years of their lives, but their concerns and conversations are those of clever children, "class brains," acting out a yearbook fantasy of adult life. (The one exception is "Tracy," the Mariel Hemingway part in *Manhattan*, another kind of adolescent fantasy. Tracy actually is a high-school senior, at the Dalton School, and has perfect skin, perfect wisdom, perfect sex, and no visible family. Tracy's mother and father are covered in a single line: they are said to be in London, finding Tracy an apartment. When Tracy wants to go to JFK she calls a limo. Tracy put me in mind of an American-International Pictures executive who once advised me, by way of pointing out the absence of adult characters in AIP beach movies, that nobody ever paid $3 to see a parent.)

Joan Didion in *The New York Review of Books*,
16 August 1979

Good luck isn't an attribute possessed by most of the cast of *Damien: Omen II*. Throughout its lacklustre and turgid length anybody who gets in the way of "The Antichrist" dies in one of the variety of ways dreamed up by the perpetrators of this latest in the seemingly endless stream of occult movies. What are they playing at, these "Producers," "Directors," "Screenwriters," "Co-Producers," "Associate Producers" and the rest? Well, clearly they're playing at making films, and I suppose rather more seriously, playing at making money.

Barry Took in *Punch*, February 1979

The nuns, as always in American films, are average American housewives inexplicably veiled in black; a twinkling bunch of good-hearted gossips, healthily unconcerned with sex. They sing all their wimples off, including—strangely enough—the Mother Superior, who bursts into full contralto shortly after informing us that singing in the cloister is forbidden.

Kenneth Tynan on *The Sound of Music*.

Proof, if proof were needed, that the return of the dumb teen comedy genre may be on its last legs, Danny Leiner's woefully inept buddy flick redefines unfunny in ways you never knew possible. Mistaking repetition of dialogue for a fruitful means of laughter grabbing, the misadventures of two stoners searching aimlessly for their missing motor takes in charmless, witless, and painfully dull in equal measures, without ever throwing in an original idea in its 82-minute running time. [...]

Risible, dire, or just about any synonym for Godawful you want to come up with... This unmitigated stream of celluloid ordure could draw a chalk outline round its corpse. All together: "Dude, where's my refund?"

William Thomas on *Dude, Where's My Car?* in
Empire magazine, issue 141, March 2001

Like Dionysus crossed with a convent girl on her first bender.
Pauline Kael on Prince's performance in
Purple Rain in *The New Yorker*, 20 August 1984

As soon as we see his chocolate-brown urchin eyes happily peering at his new wife, we know it's only a matter of time before he's bound and gagged in his underwear... This breathless demi-noir has so much bounce that we barely get any time to mull over the gaping holes in its moth-eaten plot. It is competent but extremely slight... The off-road bounces the film takes are diverting but not really unexpected; they are necessary, if only because the picture is so slight... By the end, all *Birthday Girl* does is toss off a few sparks. It doesn't generate enough down-and-dirty firepower to burst into flames.

Elvis Mitchell on *Birthday Girl* in *The New York Times*, Feb 2002

This is as slow to boil as pasta without water.

Patrick Humphries on *Barnabo of the Mountains*
in *Empire magazine*, issue 74, August 1995

Star 80 is like a pointlessly gruesome update of John
Schlesinger's *Darling*, with the very latest in smug self-
hatred. Fosse has gone so far that the question arises: Can a
movie get by with total disgust for its subject? Fosse piles
up such an accumulation of sordid scenes that the movie is
nauseated by itself.

Pauline Kael on *Star 80* in
The New Yorker, 28 November 1983

As *A Rumor of Angels* reveals itself to be a sudsy tub of super-
natural hokum, not even Ms. Redgrave's noblest efforts can
redeem it from hopeless sentimentality. [...] The story reaches
a crossroads in which it can either stay on a semi-realistic
course or flap into the mystical wild blue yonder where little
boys are touched by angels and lighthouses mysteriously flash
signals from the Great Beyond. True to form, the movie,
written by Peter O'Fallon (who directed), with James Eric and
Jamie Horton, makes the wrong choice, and out come the
flashing lights. Once it has decided to cast its lot with the
angels, it sinks (or ascends, if you will) into a humid fog of
phony, teary-eyed inspiration.

Stephen Holden on *A Rumor of Angels* in
The New York Times, 1 February 2002

Oooops, I did it again, I tested the forces of nature, and ultimately lost. After viewing the Britney Spears movie I can only say that my soul is damned, my legs are numb, and I am left with a buzzing sensation in the abdomen that I cannot explain. Now, first let it be said that it was a challenge to see the Britney movie, one that pitted movie reviewers in Kimute of sorts, except a lot less blood and a lot more inner turmoil. I can only assume that Mr. Carrichner will attempt to claim that my "love for Ms. Brit" has hardened my heart and that I only want to destroy this movie because I care so much. Let the record show that I have been bitter since 1986, way before Brit even hit the marketplace, so while I may have unresolved Tiffany issues, I am quite certain that there is no love lost between me and Britney.

Steven J. Willett on Britney Spears in *Crossroads*
at *Rant n' Rave* (www.rantrave.com)

[Wallace] Beery and [Marie] Dressler are yoked together again in *Tugboat Annie*. This film is as near a complete bore as any container of these two pleasing people could possibly be… The chief plot of the picture consists in a bad pun—Beery getting incessantly drunk; and when we are tired of laughing at this his wife gets drunk instead to give us a bit of variety.

Ivor Montagu on *Tugboat Annie*,
in the *Week-end Review*, September 1933

A bore is starred.

Village Voice review of *A Star is Born*

I should sum up the situation rather by saying that the picture was one of the poorest that Chaplin has made and that Chaplin himself, while still the best clown that the movies have bred, and while a pantomimist above the ordinary, is no longer, because of the endless repetition, anything like so amusing as once he was. In plain fact, he is frequently a bore.

George Jean Nathan on Charlie Chaplin's movie *City Lights*

Amazingly, this wretched production was financed by the BBC, which must count as the worst use of licence-payers' money since John Birt's severance package.

Philip Kemp on *Love, Honour and Obey* in *Sight and Sound*, April 2000

Hollywood in the 1930s was positively cluttered with the human flotsam of the Charles Boyer syndrome, and students of this process may have noticed how cleverly the French have recently contrived to foist Mr. Eyebrows of 1923 (Sharles Aznovoice to you) on a dismayed outside world. Every now and then we get an ugly rash of this exported Gallic charm in the movies, and it is always the same. A soundtrack so delicately adjusted that it picks up every outgoing of heavy breathing, every lick of the lips, every twitch of the labial muscles. I suppose the archetype was *A Man and a Woman*, although as I took very great care not to see that elongated commercial, I may be wrong.

Benny Green in *Punch*, 7 August 1974

...the movie, which suffers from a severe case of attention deficit disorder, is so lazy and slipshod it confuses the mere flashing of kinky soft-core imagery with naughty fun... A warning to Mr. Schwartzman: If you make any more films like *Slackers*, you could end up as this decade's answer to Pauly Shore, and that's a fate no self-respecting comic actor could wish for.

> **Stephen Holden** on *Slackers* in
> *The New York Times*, 1 February 2002

The mad-scientist subplot... is trotted out again here—with more hideous effects and loud noises than the mind can stand ladled in. Only the total collapse of Hollywood can save us from a reprise of *My Mother the Car*.

> **Kim Newman** on *My Favorite Martian*
> in *Sight and Sound*, June 1999

Probably the most unsuccessful film show was said to have occurred at the La Pampa cinema in Rio de Janeiro in November 1974.

During a screening of *The Exorcist* the audience was entirely distracted by a rat scampering to and fro before the screen. What little attention they were paying to the film was further diminished when an usherette appeared and pursued the rat with a mop.

Since this blocked the audience's view and entirely ruined a crucial vomiting scene of religious significance, the usherette was greeted with disgruntled cries of "Get them off."

Misconstruing the audience's wishes, she stunned the rat with her mop and proceeded to take all her clothes off. It was while dancing naked in the projector's light that she noticed the auditorium being cleared by armed police.

Explaining her behaviour, the usherette said afterwards, 'I thought the audience was calling for me. I was as surprised as anyone.'

Recorded by **Stephen Pile** in *The Book of Heroic Failures*
(Routledge & Keegan Paul Ltd, 1979)

Desperately Seeking Susan is a mutant of some sort, an attempt at screwball charm that can make your jaw fall open and stay down until the rest of your head joins it... When you come out of *Desperately Seeking Susan* you don't want to know who the director is—you want to know who the perpetrator is.

Pauline Kael in *The New Yorker*, 22 April 1985

The most godawful piece of pseudo-romantic slop I've ever seen! ... Even a director who had made no movies would have a hard time making one as bad as this.

Roger Ebert on *A Place for Lovers*, 1969

The picture shows glimpses of aspiring to a Graham Greene story. But as the bodies pile up and Gordy's [Arnold Schwarzenegger's] jaw becomes more deeply set, the plot is more like a Graham Cracker story—crumbly and insubstantial... Amazingly, given its brief 110-minute length, *Collateral Damage* still manages to squeeze in several different endings—like a bad pop song that doesn't know when to fade out.

Elvis Mitchell on *Collateral Damage*
in the *New York Times*, 8 February 2002

30

The only ism Hollywood believes in is plagiarism.

Dorothy Parker

"He was like an angel." Sure he was. And death isn't frightening. The only thing pumping through this Heart is rose water.

Caren Myers on *Untamed Heart* in
Sight and Sound, May 1993

This country's sad state of health care for the poor and disenfranchised is a great movie subject. Until that film comes along, we'll have to endure *John Q.*, which will leave most audiences in dire need of medical attention, though it would be hard to say if that need will come from the painful collection of plot clichés or Aaron Zigman's assaultive soundtrack. *John Q.* is a remarkable document, so ham-fisted that it sabotages its own worthwhile arguments.

Elvis Mitchell on *John Q.* in the
New York Times, 15 February 2002

The picture is a lulling, narcotizing musical; the whole damn thing throbs. It's a motorized anatomy lesson, designed to turn the kids on and drive the older men crazy. It's soft-core porn with an inspirational message, and it may be the most calculating, platinum-hearted movie I've ever seen...

It gives a hard sell even to the heroine's confessions to her priest. How tender she is, how dewy-eyed and passionate. She confesses that she has been thinking of sex, and—oh, yes—she told a lie. This girl is all underdog, and she's got a real, scene-stealing dog besides. The dog's soulful expressions have more depth than anything else in the picture.

Pauline Kael on *Flashdance* in
The New Yorker, 27 June 1983

Isn't anyone going to stick their head above the parapet and say it was pretentious twaddle? [...] Hasn't the film world, which seems to have eulogised this film all the way to the Oscar podium, got something else to say about such an empty, cold, and emotionless picture? The film imploded at its epicentre because it was guilty of the very thing it attempted to parody.

Review of *Mulholland Drive* (directed by David Lynch)
submitted by **"Philip"** to the *Guardian* web site
on 7 January 2002

With this movie you get two... two... two DiCaprios in one lame movie, wow, now that's what I call a bargain. Not only that, but you also get the lamest Musketeer story known to man... The main thrust of the story is about a bad king Louis XIV (played by a bratty DiCaprio) who spends more time wooing women than leading his country. Kind of like Clinton would be like in 17th-century France... So the next time you are considering to go see this atrocity, take a little lesson from the guys in Quiet Riot and "Bang Your Head," and I am sure that the thought will soon pass. Trust me, you'll thank me for it later.

Steven J. Willett of *Rant n Rave* (www.rantrave.com)
on *The Man in the Iron Mask*

I was surrounded by a quiet, attentive audience. People were listening to the ping-ponging vocal rhythms as if to be certain of not missing a single sinister nuance. As if you could! Every grim, frozen syllable is lobbed into your lap, along with Pinter's patented pauses—those ticktock silences that (famously) reverberate with what isn't said. The three actors all had the stricken look that is proper to a Pinter play; he doesn't bother writing about anyone who's alive. And there's nothing else going on in this movie—once you've noticed how ugly the lamps are, you're left with the stiff, stilted talk that's so calculated it's a parody. If the lines ever overlapped, it would be cataclysmic. This story of adultery told backward is a perfectly conventional corpse of a play given a ceremonious funeral on the screen. It's from Beckett by way of Terence Rattigan. Maybe not even from Beckett. When I deserted my post, the husband was acting superior and malevolent (in the Ian Holm game-playing manner), and the lover was being callow, and their eyes were darting as each watched the other's reactions. And I had got to the point of staring at their thin brown lips and wondering if the two actors had been made up with the same lipstick.

> **Pauline Kael** on *Betrayal*, the screen version of
> Harold Pinter's play of the same name.
> Reviewed in *The New Yorker*, 11 July 1983

"Can I fire you?" Scott says, by now made even more incredulous by his hapless defense attorney, and anyone sitting through this picture may feel the same way… As it is, enduring this movie feels like doing a stretch in a P.O.W. camp.

> **Elvis Mitchell** on *Hart's War* in the
> *New York Times*, 15 February 2002

I wonder what a young Israeli or Cuban would make of this profoundly parochial film: would it not astound him to be told that when the heir to the Windsor fortune contemplated marrying an American divorcée, it was "one of the most terrible decisions by which a human being has ever been confronted?" Might he not titter, or even guffaw? [...]

Home movies and international earthquakes are blandly juxtaposed, with a jarring effect of which the producer, Jack le Vien, seems raptly oblivious. Lenin addressing the workers of Russia and Mussolini leading the march on Rome are given equal screen time with the stone pelican on which young Prince Edward, in defiance of his nanny's orders, used to place funny hats.

Kenneth Tynan on *A King's Story*, a documentary
about the abdication of Edward VIII and his
marriage to Wallis Simpson.

As Swann, Jeremy Irons doesn't suggest intelligence or feeling; he's a stick, a dried-out Wasp, with dead eyes. (He couldn't be more miscast; he's out of Poe, not Proust.)

Pauline Kael on *Swann in Love* in
The New Yorker, 1 October 1984

... a feeble Sci-fi charade in which Michael York, trapped in the obligatory twenty-third century, asks a plastic surgeon to build him a new face. This is very commendable of him, as long before this happens everyone is exceedingly bored with his old one. Alas, the machine goes mad and chops up the surgeon, which is one of the very few sensible ideas in the entire scenario. Logan, I should explain, lives under one of those opaque domes which look from a distance like a boiled potato, but which turns out on closer examination actually to be a boiled potato.

Benny Green on *Logan's Run* in *Punch*, October 1976

The picture is like a slightly psychopathic version of an old Saturday-afternoon serial, with Harry sneering at the scum and cursing them before he shoots them with his king-size custom-made 44 Auto Mag. He (Clint Eastwood) takes particular pleasure in kicking and bashing a foul-mouthed lesbian; we get the idea? In his eyes, she's worse than her male associates, because women are supposed to be ladies. Eastwood's disapproval of her impropriety sits a little oddly in a movie with sub-barnyard jokes about a little bulldog's hindquarters and a laugh-fest centering on a man shot in the genitals and a frankfurter covered with ketchup.

Pauline Kael on *Sudden Impact* in *The New Yorker*, 23 January 1984.

John Book's bullet wound is healed by folk remedies: Rachel gives him herbal teas and applies poultices to the affected area. (I'm disposed to have some trust in the efficacy of these methods, but I still wish that just once somebody in a movie who was treated with humble ancient remedies would kick off.)…There's a little paradox here: *Witness* exalts people who aren't allowed to see movies—it says that they're morally superior to moviegoers. It's so virtuous it's condemning itself.

Pauline Kael on *Witness* in
The New Yorker, 25 February 1985

Cameron Crowe's *Vanilla Sky* is the feel-good movie of the year if you have just attached yourself to a Thorazine IV drip and had a Nyquil chaser. Based on the Spanish film *Abre Los Obros* (Open Your Eyes) Crowe gives us a nightmare thrill ride that is about as exciting as Webster at Epcot. ... The movie becomes Tom Cruise's *Elephant Man*, where he is not so horribly deformed but just has some minor adjustments and could still model for GQ if he had to... the horror... the horror. ... Mr. Cruise has great sexual chemistry in this film—unfortunately it is with himself... Penelope Cruz is a few *Hooked on Phonics* tapes short of being an illegal alien fry cook, she just needs to pick a language and stick with it. ... I suggest Ben & Jerry's World Famous Vanilla, it's a lot more satisfying and it whole lot easier to swallow.

Steven J. Willett of *Rant n Rave*
(www.rantrave.com) on *Vanilla Sky*

Der Rebel is a tocsin cry to the Germanic peoples to take revenge upon the French in 19— for the revenge taken by the French in 1919 for the revenge taken by the Germans in 1871 for what the French did about 1870. This barbarous vendetta-theme, which a people civilised in more than hypocritical pretence would instantly prohibit... has as little merit as a film as a speech by Hitler has as an essay in reasoned persuasion or the theory of the Aryan race has as a serious contribution to anthropology. [...] The film opens amidst exquisite Tyrolean scenery under French occupation, in an endeavour to make us forget that the French soldiers are doubtless there only because they have been persuaded that by so being they preserve somebody else from occupying possibly equally exquisite scenery back home.

Ivor Montagu on *Der Rebel*, a German Nationalist propaganda epic, in the *Week-end Review*, August 1933

The film's chief merit is an object lesson, from which we may compile a list of the rules currently governing American sex comedy; viz:

• During the time covered by the script, nobody may go to bed with anybody. This applies even to people who are married.

• Male characters must never fall in love with non-virgins.

• Female characters must never utter the word· "virgin" without stammering, or substituting, where possible, a less disgusting alternative (e.g. "beginner").

• Affairs must never be consummated. Even when the people concerned are obviously suited only to a brief liaison, they must be compelled to fall in love and marry.

• The cast should include at least one pre-war character actor to enthuse the nostalgics. [....]

• Finally, two crucial problems must be solved. First: how to get the girl wet. In *Sunday in New York* she Is drenched by a cloud-burst; in *Sex and the Single Girl*, she falls off a pier. Nothing short of a soaking is a permissible excuse for a man and a woman to remove their clothes in the same apartment. Second: how to get the girl drunk. Only tipsy heroines allow recent acquaintances to kiss them, and most film acquaintances are recent. To account for her speedy yielding, it should be explained that she has a poor head for liquor. Record for the course: "I shee what you mean," uttered by Natalie Wood in *Sex and the Single Girl* after two acorn-sized swigs.

> **Kenneth Tynan** on the Warner Brothers'
> movie *Sex and the Single Girl*

It seems that all British comedy is beginning to be afflicted by the galloping Carry Ons... Here, what we get is basically the old nineteen-thirties atmosphere of corny flatfooted British comedy animated to a certain extent by the new "permissiveness."

> **Richard Mallett** on *Doctor in Trouble*
> (which starred Leslie Phillips) in *Punch*, June 1970

If Anne Rice was upset over the film adaptation of her *Interview With the Vampire* a few years back, then she probably already has Johnnie Cochran preparing legal briefs over *Queen of the Damned*, the latest movie version of one of her books. The message of this florid and dull Queen, about the lonely ways of the undead, boils down to this: Just Say No to Blood.

> **Elvis Mitchell** on *Queen of the Damned* in *The New York Times*, 22 February 2002

The not noticeably Greek Christian Bale is so wooden he seems intent on a one-man impersonation of Epping Forest.

> **Christoper Tookey** on *Captain Corelli's Mandolin* in the *Daily Mail*

Ben Hur belongs to a certain cinematic genre, which makes it much easier to define. If I say that it is by *Quo Vadis* out of *The Robe* you will immediately get the feel of that dreadful clammy evangelising in which Hollywood will sometimes indulge when it feels in urgent need of a fast buck.

> **Benny Green** in *Punch*, March 1977

This is a movie about a young Hungarian who prefers making love to older Hungarian women, does so, becomes involved in the 1956 Hungarian revolution (he says), leaves Hungary, goes to Canada and there makes love to older Canadian women. It's a film that flaps on leaden wings from one bedroom scene to another with all the grace of a comatose rhinoceros (a flying rhino? It must be the work of the devil) and is not illuminating, titillating, or interesting.

Barry Took on *In Praise of Older Women* in
Punch, February 1979

This dingy charade spends two hours repeating a message already familiar in the first twenty minutes: "All they want is my body." Carroll Baker supplies the body, if not the erotic incandescence that made them want it. "She didn't die of pneumonia," says her agent after the girl gasps her last, "she died of life." In fact, she died of neither. Nothing reveals the essential mendacity of Harlow more clearly than its refusal to admit that a Hollywood sex symbol could die of uremic poisoning. Angela Lansbury, Raf Vallone, and Red Buttons are among those who officiate at this shoddy exhumation.

Kenneth Tynan on a "biopic" of the
Hollywood actress Jean Harlow

A great tragedy suffocated by tyrannical sentimentality.

Andrew O'Hehir on *The Perfect Storm* in
Sight and Sound, September 2000

Frankly, I thought it was tripe designed and made quite brilliantly for an audience of village idiots.

Barry Took on *Close Encounters of the Third Kind*,
in *Punch at the Cinema* (1981)

These zombies would rather lie on the sofa watching MTV eating cheesy snacks than consume human flesh.

Kim Newman on *Idle Hands* in *Sight and Sound*, June 2000

Although the drama that storms across this rugged paradise encompasses a war and a major earthquake, not to mention oodles of star-crossed love, little of it comes to life... as the movie methodically plods forward on a screenplay (by Shawn Slovo) consisting entirely of clichés and watered-down exposition, it becomes sadly apparent that its only reliable asset is the gorgeous view. [...]

Of the three principals, Mr. Bale [as Mandras] is the most comfortable speaking in a foreign accent... But probably no actor could transcend the turgid romantic mush stuffed into the mouths of these three. The inevitable after-the-war reunion scene between two of them is so clumsily written and played as to be laughable.

Stephen Holden on *Captain Corelli's Mandolin* in
The New York Times on 17 August 2001

Tim Burton has now become a problem; I still find myself watching his movies with bemused tolerance, thinking surely he'll be a great director when he grows up. Although it's loaded with pseudo-ghoulish detail and imbued with a distinctive atmosphere... *Sleepy Hollow* suffers from terminal vagueness and clutter.

Andrew O'Hehir in *Sight and Sound*, February 2000

One of the most curious features of daily life in the past few years has been the amazing comeback of Mickey Mouse, who has so speedily and so utterly become the vest-fronting, car-sticking talisman of the age, almost as though the adult world, finally confused beyond rational thought by the ecological conundrums of the modern era, had decided to clutch to its bosom the most reassuring symbol it could find of the sweets of childhood.

Benny Green in *Punch*, 5 December 1973

Absolutely disgusting.

The first known film review—of a picture called *May Irwin Kiss*—in the *Chap Book*, 15 June 1896

The movie is of an unbelievable badness; it brings back clichés you didn't know you knew… You can't get angry at something this stupefying; it seems to have been made by trolls.

Pauline Kael on *Song of Norway*, a biopic of the composer Edvard Grieg, 1970

To be fair, the movie does show a certain charm in its relent-lessly stupid grasp of the obvious. When Frampton sings "The Long and Winding Road," for example, he is walking down a long and winding road. You keep laughing and thinking it can't get any worse. But it does.

Charles M. Young on the Beatles' movie *Sergeant Pepper's Lonely Heart Club Band*, in *Rolling Stone* magazine, 1978

After three hours you are just barely holding onto your senses after seeing a barrage of images and some of the worst dialogue in years... If you have any love of the game, forget this movie, it will not help. If you sort of like the game, don't even bother, it will just turn you off. And if you are like me and just watch the Super Bowl for the Doritos commercials, then this movie is practically the worst thing that you can spend $8.50 and three hours on.

> **Steven J. Willett** of *Rant n Rave* (www.rantrave.com)
> on the football movie *Any Given Sunday*

L.A. Without a Map is one piece of celluloid that deserves to get lost.

> **Melanie McGrath** in *Sight and Sound*, October 1999

With pseudo-suave repartee that would make Austin Powers blush and with so many shades of "Howard the Duck" that one scene depicts man-size pastel teddy bears sitting around a conference table, it's a film to gall fans of the old television series and perplex anyone else. I can't remember another Friday morning show where I heard actual cries of "Ugh!" on the way out the door.

With a perfect lack of chemistry between them, Uma Thurman and Ralph Fiennes play Mrs. Peel and John Steed, the woman in the catsuit and the man who fights boldly with his umbrella. To put it mildly, the dandified Fiennes does not look capable of inflicting serious damage with that bumbershoot, and Ms. Thurman had a better costume-party role as Poison Ivy in *Batman Forever*. Also in the cast, as a madman scheming grandly to control the weather, is Sean Connery. Connery has what is surely the silliest line of his entire, distinguished career: "Rain or shine, it's all mine!" Dressed and wigged in mock-glamorous fashion, Connery has never looked more like Burt Reynolds. […]

At a pared-down, barely rational 100 minutes, *The Avengers* is short but not short enough.

Janet Maslin on *The Avengers* in
The New York Times on 15 August 1998

Alvin tells a sad runaway a little homily about binding sticks together into a bunch so they won't break. "That's family," he sums up; at which point, ill-natured viewers will snarl that the Romans used to call such wooden bundles *fasces* and look where that homely symbol ended up.

Kevin Jackson on *The Straight Story* in
Sight and Sound December 1999

Critics are always being told that their only duty is to decide whether a given work is "good of its kind." But there are kinds that were never meant to be "good," by anyone's definition of art. They are commodities, articles made with no thought of lasting, designed solely to be bought and consumed. Pace the supporters of pop art, those panicky propagandists who believe that the only way to give art a place in a profit-based world is to erase the vital boundary between art and commerce, the wrapper around a can of soup cannot be judged on artistic terms. Nor likewise, can *Where Love Has Gone*, before which criticism retires, yielding place to astounded resumé, with sociological footnotes.

In the words of the song, love walked right in and puked all over the floor; but not as wholeheartedly as in this "blistering best-seller" by Harold Robbins, brought to the screen (for those who like to be blistered) by the team who cleaned up with *The Carpet-Baggers*, an earlier work from the same pen. [...]

It is here (or hereabouts: who can swear to the time-sequence of events in a nightmare?) that the great lines proliferate. Miss Davis to Miss Hayward: "You have devoted your life to mud and filth." Mr. Connors to Miss Hayward: "You're not a woman, you're a disease." Miss Hayward's daughter (a pouting brat) to a psychologist who confronts her with proof that she has lost her virginity: "It could have happened horseback riding." Miss Davis, on hearing that her daughter and grand-daughter are being blackmailed because they slept with the same man: "To have one hundred years of social standing brought to earth in a mass of feathers!" (That may originally have read "a mess of feathers;" Miss Davis has been known to lengthen her vowels in moments of emotional stress). The picture ends with Miss Hayward driving off in a swell of hopeful music to a State institution. Direction by Edward Dmytryk, with dresses by Edith Head. Miss Head deserves congratulation.

Kenneth Tynan on *Where Love Has Gone*,
which starred Bette Davis

Despite a great soundtrack, watching *54* is more like swallowing a bottle of quaaludes: let's hope it's the last stop on the current nostalgia trip.

Liese Spencer on *54* in *Sight and Sound*,
February 1999

Take a rich boy and a poor girl, give one of them a terminal illness, drip slurpy string music all over the soundtrack, have them cavort in wonderful costumes around beautiful surroundings, and throw in high-art references, and you have *Love Story*

rethought for the 90s, with the rich guy going bald from leukemia chemotherapy this time and the poor girl sticking by him to the last, and Julia Roberts demonstrating her undeniable star power and unerring eye for truly terrible scripts. [...]

Dying Young is batting fair to be reckoned the Worst Film Of 1991. Avoiding all the obvious shortcuts like being a sequel or a low-budget slasher film, it manages to be absolutely excruciating on a big budget, with a talented cast, an agonisingly contrived visual style and a supposedly sure-fire premise. If nothing else, this ought to be a three-hankie weeper for patrons who leave their brains behind, but actually all the emotional contrivances and tearful scenes turn annoyingly gigglesome as the paper thin characters whine at each other. [...]

Meanwhile, donate the ticket money you would have spent to medical research, and stay home.

Jack Yeovil on *Dying Young* in
Empire magazine, issue 28, October 1991

This extravagant, meandering piece of whimsy.
Geoffrey Macnab on *Meet Joe Black* in
Sight and Sound, February 1999

The Astronaut's Wife arrived Friday in a veil of mystery. How could a thriller starring Johnny Depp and Charlize Theron be so bad that New Line Cinema, which has been in no hurry to release this film, would not risk screening in advance for the press?

Answer: as directed by Rand Ravich, it's actually a lot better than these circumstances suggest. But as written by Ravich, a screenwriter directing his debut feature, *The Astronaut's Wife* is ridiculously derivative...

This film's answer to the question of whether there is intelligent life elsewhere in the universe: not too.

Janet Maslin on *The Astronaut's Wife* in
The New York Times on 28 August 1999

I had never numbered Bergman among the slyer contemporary wags; all the same, I expected something slightly less elephantine than tinted Norman Wisdom. "What goings-on! I gape in amazement," remarks one of the subtitles, and I can't say I blame it.

Kenneth Tynan on *Now About These Women*
by Ingmar Bergman

The film drags on for more than two hours before Winkler signs off with yet another of the film's endless crane shots —the camera soars into the air as the couple walk away into the distance, an appropriately cornball ending for a film which feels contrived and phoney from start to finish.

Geoffrey Macnab on *At First Sight* in
Sight and Sound, June 1999

The transformation of *The Last of the Mohicans* into *Adirondack Vice* is thus a successful and international disaster.

Henry Sheehan in *Sight and Sound*, November 1992

Of *Every Which Way But Loose*... I hesitate to speak. It stars Clint Eastwood as a genial bare-fist fighter with a pet Orang-Utan, a friend, and a fantasy about a girl country-and-western singer.

There are jokes in it and fist fights, a moment or two of mild sex, some songs in the country-and-western manner, and it's absolute and complete nonsense. Not that it isn't viewable. It is. But like the wine buff who says it makes a refreshing change to drink a really bad wine, so *Every Which Way But Loose* makes a refreshing change from a surfeit of "good" movies.

Barry Took in *Punch*, January 1979

Continually labouring to top the last gag, they run the risk of expiring on successive doses of their own poison.

Xan Brooks on *Very Bad Things* in
Sight and Sound, January 1999

THIS this THIS this THIS is the kind of THING (from outer SPACE?) you can expect from *Help!*, the new (and BAM!! it's new or never) film directed by focus-pulling, prize-winning, gag-spawning, zoom-loving Richard ("The KNACK") Lester, shot (POWWW!) in Eastmancolour but influenced by Observacolour and suggesting whole libraries of colourmags sprung BOING! to instant obsolescent life, complete with COOL gaudy consumer-tailored featurettes (one Lester missed: "Tread Softly: The Dream-World of Wall-To-Wall Carpeting") and genuine only-connecting ADS (another Lester missed: "Why not fly to the Aleutians in your custom-built Hammond Organ?"), not to mention FOUR EXPENSIVE TWO-DIMENSIONAL OBJECTS— namely John Lennon, the snickering heavyweight punster; surly, bejewelled Ringo Starr; George Harrison, the 12-string narcissist;

and Paul McCartney, the boy next fibre-glass-electric-eye-operated door (under that wig he's really—GASP!—Anne Rutherford)—who are flung about (URGGHH!), battered (SPLAT!!) and flattened (KER-PLUNK!!!) in a comic-strip chase through tourist-enticing London, the whiter-than-white Austrian Alps, and selected sunsoaked Bahamas, pursued by Oriental goodness-gracious villains (" 'It's a Sellers' market,' quips writer Charles Wood") and guaranteed mad scientists, all plotting to slice (EEK!) a magic ring from surly Ringo's bejewelled finger, while off-beat Lester movie garners harvest of heady hosannas ("LOFTY GROSSES LOOM FOR MOPHEADS" LATEST—Flicker's Total Sexlessness Augers Wham Family Fare') from notoriously hard-to-please CRITICS (ECCHH!!) in American trade press…

Kenneth Tynan on the Beatles' movie *Help!* (directed by Richard Lester).

I'm sure pictures like this give people pimples.

Pauline Kael on *Sweet November*

Marilyn Monroe was so minimally gifted as to be unemployable.

Clive James

[It has] all the profundity of a dial tone.

Stephanie Zacharek on *Hanging Up* in *Sight and Sound*, May 2000

48

The pitch must have gone something like this. "It's *The Firm* on Campus! It's *The Game* meets *Dawson's Creek*! It's got rowing for the sports fans and Joshua Jackson in spandex for the Joshua Jackson in spandex fans! It's all about power and privilege being brought low by an ordinary Joe. It's a can't fail!'

Tragically, this heady brew does indeed fail on almost every level, for screenwriter Pogue and director Cohen have delivered what is simply the most ferociously stupid movie that Hollywood has disgorged in a long time. Indeed, there's a perverse masochistic pleasure to be had in hanging around just to see how much dumber it can get. And on that level, this just keeps giving. [...]

The performances are uniformly dismal, with Jackson delivering a turn of such stupefying, lumber-like uselessness that you get the feeling that if the supposed teen ever gets cagey about his real age, we could simply saw him in half and count the rings. But it's Pogue's script that really excels itself.

The idiocies are legion, but there's the fact that the society is so fantastically secret that it has a huge, illuminated skull on its roof. Then there's the Frankenstein's castle-like Skull HQ, where whenever you press a light switch, flaming torches ignite on the walls. Plus the fact that, with its rowing theme, this was probably titled "Sculls" originally, but Americans didn't get it. Unutterable tommyrot.

Adam Smith on *The Skulls* in
Empire magazine, issue 138, December 2000

28 Days is not bad enough to ruin your life, nor is it good enough to change it even remotely. In any event, you won't need more than an hour to recover from it.

Stephanie Zacharek in *Sight and Sound*, June 2000

She has only two expressions—joy and indigestion.
Dorothy Parker on the film star Marion Davies

The entertainment value is akin to watching war newsreel while someone shines a bright light in your eye.
Philip J. Kaplan on *Xanadu*, 1983

I rate this a 10. I like David Lynch. But if one doesn't like being locked in a cage for two hours and poked with a stick by someone who just wants to get a reaction out of you, then you should subtract anywhere from 8-10 points from this review.
Review of *Mulholland Drive* (directed by David Lynch) by **"Paul"** on the *Guardian* web site, November 2001

There are more thrills to be found in the average dolphinarium.
Sight and Sound magazine on *Orca...Killer Whale*, 1977

I still can't believe I saw this freak show, a self-consciously mod, disjointed patchwork of leers, vulgarity, and general ineptness.
William Wolf on *Myra Breckenridge* in *Cue*, 1970

Awful... the worst experience I ever had in a cinema.

Gary Arnold on *The Music Lovers*, a biopic of the
composer Tchaikovsky, played by Richard Chamberlain,
in the *Washington Post*, 1970

A picture of which it might be said they shouldn't make 'em like
that any more.

Robert Hatch on *The Missouri Breaks*,
which starred Marlon Brando and Jack Nicholson,
in *Nation*, 1976

Even the title of *I Still Know What You Did Last Summer* doesn't bear
thinking about.

Kim Newman in *Sight and Sound*, May 1999

Marlon Brando at 52 has the sloppy belly of a 62-year-old, the
white hair of a 72-year-old, and the total lack of discipline of a
precocious 12-year-old.

The Sun on *The Missouri Breaks*, 1976

Another nostalgic pipeline to the 1930s was opened last week,
with the presentation of *The Best of Busby Berkeley*—an
anthology of production numbers devised and directed by a man
summed up in the credit titles as "the Master Builder of the

American Musical Film." Berkeley's was the era when crooners whistled, wore billowing trousers, and were usually Dick Powell; when chorus girls danced on acres of shiny black floor; were constantly caught in the rain, played neon-lit violins, formed jigsaw puzzles of the American flag, wore hooped tortillas of satin, waltzed on serpentine staircases, slid down water-chutes like medieval sinners on their way to hell, and—the Berkeley trademark par excellence—were shot from above in concentric circles, at once floral and anal in design.

Kenneth Tynan on *The Best of Busby Berkeley*

As uplifting as a whalebone bra—and just as dated.

Arthur Cooper on *Lost Horizon* in *Newsweek*, 1972

The most hilariously maladroit historical pageant since King David—this movie is nuts.

Village Voice on *Revolution*, which starred Al Pacino, 1985

It's… possible that the world would be a better place if no one went to see *Collateral Damage* (Warner Bros.)… it's another dumb vengeance picture—*In the Bedroom* for meatheads.

David Edelstein in *Slate* on *Collateral Damage*, 8 February 2002

After a while this had the feel of a very poorly made Woody Allen movie as the characters barely made any attempts to develop into real people… There are a couple of lessons to be learned from this film.

1. If you are gay and like Jennifer Aniston, she will eventually fall in love with you and have to break off the friendship.

2. Jennifer Aniston evidently cannot turn a gay man straight.

3. And, finally, John Pankow should stay with TV sitcoms.

> **Steven J. Willett** of *Rant n Rave* (www.rantrave.com)
> on *The Object of My Affection*

The sea-picture is really a cowboy film in which all the cows are sea-cows.

> **Ivor Montagu** on *Below the Sea*, in the
> *Week-end Review*, October 1933

Here's a word of travel advice for all of you frequent flyers out there: if you are planning on taking a trip for a nice relaxing time, first find out where Leonardo DiCaprio is going and then pick the furthest possible place on Earth. Yes Leo is back on the big screen and if you thought he was just an over-hyped and overpriced megalomaniac bratty star, well then you would be correct… Want to see what happens when Club Med goes bad, then *The Beach* might be for you.

> **Steven J. Willett** of *Rant n Rave* (www.rantrave.com)

Havers has a unique twist in the old "take me to your leader routine" in which he splutters "Look, I'm a Serving British Officer!" prior to offering fags round the native company (who understandably tie him up when he's asleep) while Nolte appears to have based his performance on the bearded castaway who intermittently staggers onto shot during *The Monty Python's Flying Circus*.

> **Lloyd Bradley** on *Farewell to the King*, which starred Nigel Havers, in *Empire* magazine, issue 1, June 1989

All that's left is for the audience to identify the corpse of a good idea.

> **Liese Spencer** on *Random Hearts* in *Sight and Sound*, December 1999

La Peau Douce is François Truffaut's bid for the major circuits, and its glossy banality will bring comfort to those beleaguered malcontents who thought *Jules et Jim* an inflated romantic bore. A stodgy and charmless literary man (Jean Desailly) has an affair with a sexy air hostess whom he takes so much for granted that she deserts him—too late, however, to prevent his wife from seizing a rifle and mowing him down in a restaurant. Laced with irony, this anecdote might have been bearable; instead, Truffaut gives it the full sentimental treacle (nobody bats an eyelid without waking up the entire studio orchestra) and pads it to a length of two hours with every cliché in the book, including repeated expositions in close-up of how to start and stop a car and how to make a telephone call. *La Peau Douce* is the sort of picture that Hollywood used to turn out twenty-five years ago. I can see the hoardings now: *They Met in the Clouds*, co-starring George Brent and Ann Sheridan.

Kenneth Tynan

What kind of a title for a movie is *Greystoke: The Legend of Tarzan, Lord of the Apes*? A pompous, foolish one. There can't be many people who will remember this title, or many theatres that are equipped with colons for their marquees, either.

Pauline Kael in *The New Yorker*, 2 April 1984

The main lesson to be learned here is "don't go out with U.S. Marshals unless you are sure you can seduce them and they won't call for backup." Do they make the big score? Will they beat the thugs to the diamonds? Will Karen and Foley ever get together? How many licks does it takes to get to the center of a Tootsie Roll Pop? Some of these questions are answered, but after seeing long periods of waiting in cars, waiting in apartments, and more chit chat, you really do not care all that much.

… alas, this movie drags like a solar powered racecar during an eclipse… As the saying goes, "Out of sight, out of mind" and I couldn't agree more heartily.

Steven J. Willett of *Rant n Rave* (www.rantrave.com) on *Out of Sight*, which starred George Clooney and Jennifer Lopez

Literature

His verse exhibits... something that is rather like Keats's vulgarity with a Public School accent.

F. R. Leavis referring to Rupert Brooke
New Bearings in English Poetry, Ch. 2

Have you got Boswell's most absurd enormous book?—the best thing in it is a *bon mot* of Lord Pembroke. The more one learns of Johnson, the more preposterous assemblage he appears of strong sense, of the lowest bigotry and prejudices, of pride, brutality, fretfulness and vanity—and Boswell is the ape of most of his faults, without a grain of his sense. It is the story of a mountebank and his zany.

Horace Walpole on James Boswell's *Life of Johnson*

Science fiction is no more written for scientists than ghost stories are written for ghosts.

Brian Aldiss, introduction to Penguin Science Fiction

Some books are to be tasted, others to be swallowed, and some few to be chewed.

Francis Bacon, 1st Baron Verulam,
Viscount St. Albans, Essays, "Of Studies"

We were put to Dickens as children but it never quite took. That unremitting humanity soon had me cheesed off.

Alan Bennett, *The Old Country II*

English, being the language of an imaginative race, abounds in clichés, so that English literature is always in danger of being poisoned by its own secretions.

Gerald Brenan, *Thoughts in a Dry Season*, "Literature"

The Fleshly School of Poetry.

Robert Williams Buchanan, referring to Swinburne, William Morris, D. Rossetti, etc. Title of article in the *Contemporary Review*, Oct 1871

The misfortune is, that he has begun to write verses without very well understanding what metre is.

Samuel Taylor Coleridge, referring to Tennyson, *Table Talk*

As a piece of good taste [his essay on George Sterling] ranks with that statuette of the Milo Venus with the clock in her stomach.

Dorothy Parker on Upton Sinclair in *The New Yorker*, December 1927

Books are made not like children but like pyramids… and they're just as useless! And they stay in the desert! … Jackals piss at their foot and the bourgeois climb up on them.

Gustave Flaubert, Letter to Ernest Feydeau, 1857

A book may be amusing with numerous errors, or it may be very dull without a single absurdity.

Oliver Goldsmith, Advertisement for *The Vicar of Wakefield*

The work of Henry James has always seemed divisible by a simple dynastic arrangement into three reigns: James I, James II, and the Old Pretender.

Philip Guadella, Collected Essays, "*Men of Letters: Mr. Henry James,*" 1920

In my opinion, even the *Dialogues of Plato* drag. They are over-written, and I regret that a man who had many better things to say wasted so much time in long and needless preliminary conversations.

Montaigne

I am also writing a preface for an American edition of Galsworthy's *Man of Property*. Ever read it? Don't. He was the last English novelist to be granted general reverence. He is really shockingly dull. I had the hope that it was youthful snobbery which made me despise him. But no. He's no good.

Evelyn Waugh in a letter to Ann Fleming, 7 August 1963. From *The Letters of Evelyn Waugh* (1980)

Chuang Tzu was born in the fourth century before Christ. The publication of his book in English, two thousand years after his death, is obviously premature.

Anonymous

[He] was widely hailed as one of the greatest of American realists and as one of the finest American novelists. In this last year I have undertaken, in the services of truth and the national honor, to read again every book that he wrote, and I emerge from that grand plunge with the conviction that, if here was an important realistic mind and an important novelist, I am either the poorest judge of intellectual and literary values this side of Columbia University or one whom the wholesale reading in question has paralyzed out all possibly nascent critical talent.

George Jean Nathan on David Graham Phillips

Books are fatal: they are the curse of the human race. Nine-tenths of existing books are nonsense, and the clever books are the refutation of that nonsense. The greatest misfortune that ever befell man was the invention of printing.

Benjamin Disraeli

And it is that word "hummy," my darlings, that marks the first place in *The House at Pooh Corner* at which Tonstant Weader Fwowed up.

Dorothy Parker—who reviewed for *The New Yorker* under the pseudonym "Constant Reader"—on the "hums" of Pooh in *The House at Pooh Corner* by A. A. Milne. In *The New Yorker*, October 1928

A classic is something that everybody wants to have read and nobody wants to read.

Mark Twain

It is impossible not to feel that Mr. James has at last contrived to write a dull book. *The Portrait of a Lady* is of enormous length, being printed much more closely than is usual with three-volume novels; and a large part of it is made up of page after page of narrative and description, in which the author goes on refining and distinguishing, as if unable to hit on the exact terms necessary to produce the desired effect.

The Athanaeum (no. 2822), 26 November 1881

An enthusiasm for Poe is the mark of a decidedly primitive stage of reflection.

Henry James on the poet Edgar Allen Poe

Given that the history of the world can in a sense be seen as a history of the difficult men who have run it, it seems appropriate to register a protest against Mr. Plante's title. No one has yet written a book about three moderately famous men who happened to know each other and called it "Difficult Men." (Or even "Nice Men: A Memoir of Three.") Still, there's no sense in being curmudgeonly, or in pretending that there's no such thing as a difficult woman—the chances are that if you aren't "difficult" no one will write a book about you. Mr. Plante is very good at describing some of the ways in which women can make life hard, while insinuating that no merit attaches to being friends with someone it's easy to be friends with. "Difficult women," it turns out, can make you like yourself better for liking them.

Mary-Kay Wilmers on *Difficult Women: A Memoir of Three* by David Plante, in the *London Review of Books*, 1983

※

What are American dry-goods? American novels.

Oscar Wilde

※

Having never had any mental vision, he has now lost his bodily sight; a silly coxcomb, fancying himself a beauty; an unclean beast, with nothing more human about him than his guttering eyelids; the fittest doom for him would be to hang him on the highest gallows, and set his head on the Tower of London.

Salmasius (Claude de Saumaise) on the poet John Milton

※

I was never allowed to read the popular American children's books of my day because, as my mother said, the children spoke bad English without the author's knowing it.

Edith Wharton

※

Mr. Sinclair Lewis is a very robust writer; he delights in what Mr. Wells has called "The jolly little coarsenesses of life," and he finds crime more excusable than the present American system of suppressing crime. At his best, his humour and high spirits atone for his vulgarity; at this worst, his apparent dread of decency makes his book very depressing.

L. P. Hartley on *Ann Vickers* by Sinclair Lewis in the *Week-end Review*, January 1933

Idle books get born because people don't attend to their proper business, but leap at the chance to divert themselves from it.

Montaigne

One must have a heart of stone to read the death of Little Nell without laughing.

Oscar Wilde on Dickens's *The Old Curiosity Shop*

It may be that this autobiography is set down in sincerity, frankness, and simple effort. It may be, too, that the Statue of Liberty is situated in Lake Ontario.

Dorothy Parker on evangelist Aimee Semple McPherson's autobiography, entitled *In the Service of the King*, in *The New Yorker*, February 1928

The general verdict on *Bleak House* and such like, showed that even Mr. Dickens could not make novels with a popular purpose in England.

The Contemporary Review, vol. 11, August 1869

Perhaps I have hit on a reason for my waning love of novels of which I was not aware before—that they have substituted gynaecology for romance.

Ben Hecht, quoted in Bartlett's *Unfamiliar Quotations* (1972)

Levin's odyssey through his own greed is aggressive and ridiculous. He may see himself as busy slaying the New Puritans, but it is the story really of his own appetite that concerns him… I am drawn to his hope of glimpsing into transcendental things, but most of this offensive book is accusatory: if you don't talk big, and think big, like Levin, you are somehow anti-life. Why should we be told about his eating something, stuffed with something else, sauté'd in some other bloody thing, and dished up in some unreachable village in Provence that no one else knows about? Does it matter that Bernard Levin is surprised that he didn't discover (or is it invent?) Shakespeare until he was 11? He tells us that "a man of modest means" may not "be able to eat at the Gavroche, but he can eat at the Gay Hussar." You have only to ponder what a family of modest means would make of that to see it for the baloney that it is. Books like this drive one to class warfare, simply as a way of answering back.

Michael Neve on Bernard Levin's *Enthusiasms*, in the *London Review of Books*, 1985

I can't tell you that I think *The Man Who Knew Coolidge*, whether regarded as an entertainment, a portrait, a contribution to American letters, or as all three, is rotten. I could say that if I could use the word "rotten," but I can't use the word "rotten." The question of honor is involved. I gave my solemn pledge that I wouldn't say "rotten" any more. "Rotten" is not a nice word for a lady to use. It sounds lousy.

But I can say—and, if you don't mind, I will—that I think Mr. Lewis's latest work is as heavy-handed, clumsy, and dishonest a burlesque as it has been my misfortune to see in years. I say it, I admit, waiting for a bolt of lightening to come and flatten me permanently, for it is dangerous business for the likes of me to go about saying harsh things of Sinclair Lewis… I am trembling like a what's-this leaf for my presumption, but I stick to my story.

Dorothy Parker on *The Man Who Knew Coolidge* by Sinclair Lewis in *The New Yorker*, April 1928

Taken one by one, each of these stories is prettily fashioned enough: fluently written, finely observed, dextrously assembled, but in the end, a little slight—a little too cerebral to be affecting, a little too banal to be intellectually compelling.

Michiko Kakutani on *Cross Channel stories* by Julian Barnes.
The New York Times, April 16, 1996

In a way, the main fault of all books is that they are too long.
Luc de Clapier Vauvenargues

In renouncing her gift for psychological insight and social detail, Ms. Lurie has produced a thin, spindly novel, peopled not by flesh and blood characters but by papery cartoons. Her wicked sense of humor, once used to point up the absurdities of contemporary life, is now employed solely at her characters' expense, just as her cool omniscience has given way to a chilly, sardonic detachment.

Michiko Kakutani on *The Last Resort* by Alison Lurie.
The New York Times, 3 July 1998

She betrays her unfamiliarity with the mere letter as well as the spirit of poetic art, and makes blunders in versification, which cannot be blamed without some apparent petulance in the critic; for perfection of mechanical execution in a modern poem is so entirely taken for granted, that the charge of failure in this respect looks much like ungenerous carping, and is received with liberal incredulity. But even a careless reader of "The Spanish Gypsy" could not fail to note how many lines have but four feet, or four feet and a half, and how little is done to restore the lost balance by giving other lines five and a half, six, and even seven feet.

Review of "The Spanish Gypsy: A Poem" by George Eliot, in *The Atlantic Monthly*, Vol. 22, 1868

Too-too awful!

Punch's verdict of a poem by Oscar Wilde (he is also given the nickname "Oscuro Wildegoose"), 20 August 1881

Denied a thematic thread to pull him through, the reader is not allowed even to follow chronology. Each chapter doubles back and forth among the centuries. You no sooner settle to North American women pretend-naives of circa 1845 than the next paragraph knocks you back to 17th-century Ravenna. The hypothesis is unavoidable that Ms Greer committed her researches to a card index in which some natural catastrophe shuffled the entries and destroyed the divider cards before the entries were transcribed. Ms Greer's most succinct descriptive writing is in the title of her book, which characterises the text with precision.

Brigid Brophy on *The Obstacle Race* by Germaine Greer in the *London Review of Books*, 22 November 1979

For, however full of sweetness and beauty of feeling and richness of words these books are, even love must labor strenuously through them, and a crude surfeit reigns. Often, too, their stories are almost lost in the telling. Yes, to be sure it is good to have wide fields to delay and wander in sometimes, to feel our feet tangled in soft luxuries of grass, and turn backward and sideways to pluck posies; but the longest way around is not the nearest way home for the true artist, when he wishes to lodge himself securely overnight in the heart of his reader. He may find that far-off, invisible person tired of waiting (there are many long-sitting, and long-suffering readers, nevertheless), with the door shut, the light put out, and – is he musing or asleep?

Review of *The Earthly Paradise* by William Morris
in *The Atlantic Monthly*, Vol. 25, 1870

He has no talent for compression, nor any of that precision of touch which enables Tolstoy to make a mass of detail interesting and significant. In the small piece, frankly, he is an unattractive writer.

L. P. Hartley on *A Gallery of Women* by Theodore Dreiser
in *The Week-end Review*, April 1930

E. M. Forster never gets any further than warming the teapot. He's a rare fine hand at that. Feel this teapot. Is it not beautifully warm? Yes, but there ain't going to be no tea.

Katherine Mansfield, diary entry, May 1917

Mr. James's style has been praised both duly and unduly. It abounds in implications, in subtleties; there are delicate touches of recording observation; there is frequent cleverness of phrase, though these ingenuities are sometimes pressed to the impairment of the meaning. A more serious defect of it is a certain labored quality, a certain lack of spontaneity. It is the reverse in this respect of Thackeray's, for instance. It reminds us, too often for full enjoyment, of a well attired person who is somewhat uneasily conscious of his dress. The last secret of literary style, the ars celare artem, is still a secret for Mr. James to master.

The Independent (no. 30) on Henry James's novel
The Europeans, 21 November 1878

Mr. Henry James writes fiction as if it were a painful duty.
Oscar Wilde

❧

Reading him is like wading through glue.
Alfred Lord Tennyson on Ben Jonson

❧

This will never do.
Francis, Lord Jeffrey on William Wordswoth's poem
The Excursion (1814) in the *Edinburgh Review*, November 1814

❧

It is owing, no doubt, to a greater difference in the constitution of society in France that, judged by the rules regulating our social life, many French books written with a manifest moral purpose are immoral to us, because the improper is made so very conspicuous when absent. In situations where the Anglo-Saxon would not suspect, Lamartine, for instance, in his most impossible Platonic stories, is sure to tell with gratuitous solemnity that everything was perfectly correct. If Monsieur Sylvestre, therefore, is not free from this species of negative impurity, it would appear to be not so much the fault of Madame Dudevant as of her nation and its literature.
Review of *Monsieur Sylvestre*, a novel by George Sand, in *The Atlantic Monthly*, Vol. 26, 1870

❧

The scientific machinery is not very delicately constructed, and the imagination of the reader is decidedly overtaxed.
Review of *The Invisible Man* by H. G. Wells in *The New York Times Book Review*, 25 December 1897

[*Frankenstein* is] a book about what happens when a man tries to have a baby without a woman.

> **Anne K. Mellor** on Mary Shelley's novel in
> the *Sunday Correspondent*, 8 April 1990

It is difficult to imagine the kind of reader who will look forward with pleasure to two more sections of this unpleasant book. To many Agnostics its treatment of a future state and the judgement of souls will afford an example of deplorable taste, while to any conceivable kind of Christian it will be ribald blasphemy.

> *The English Review*, August 1928, on
> *The Childermass* by Wyndham Lewis

Mr. Flaubert is an author who has won considerable reputation in France by three novels which have already called out a great deal of discussion, both in the country where they were written and elsewhere; they are *Madame Bovary*, *L'Éducation Sentimentale*, and *Salammbô*. In all of them there was talent of a certain kind, enough to get itself very much talked about, but chiefly from the novelty of the author in maintaining the paradox that the treatment of any subject, if only clever, could outweigh the most natural objections to a distasteful topic.

> **Comment** on the French author Gustave Flaubert
> in *The Atlantic Monthly*, Vol. 34, 1874

One should not be too severe on English novels; they are the only relaxation of the intellectually unemployed.

> **Oscar Wilde** in the *Pall Mall Gazette*, 4 August 1886

We find his novels extolled as agreeable and wholesome, but it is hard to assent conscientiously to either adjective. To our thinking, the present attempt is not only carried out with the least possible energy, either as to representation of character or as to the invention of the simplest incident, but it is also extremely fatiguing reading, and in portions decidedly repulsive, owing to the author's total want of inspiration when handling unpleasant episodes. The feebleness of his imagination, too, causes the more emotional parts to sound like burlesque. All these defects are not new in Mr. Trollope's work, but, together with his amazing repetitional prolixity, they are becoming very tiresome.

Review of *The Prime Minister* by Anthony Trollope
in *The Atlantic Monthly*, Vol. 38, 1876

Common sense about Women is the title of a book lately published. Grampus says it ought to consist of one Chapter, and that that Chapter should be in one sentence (after the manner of the celebrated Chapter on Snakes in Ireland), namely, "There is no common sense about Women!"

Punch review from October 1882

A philosophising serpent... that hyena in petticoats.
Horace Walpole on Mary Wollstonecraft, *Letters*, 1798

It is far better to be silent than merely to increase the quantity of bad books.

Voltaire

He [Lord Byron] writes like a housewife on the verge of the vapors.

Robert Bolt

The Ancient Mariner would not have been taken so well if it had been called The Old Sailor.

Samuel Butler

There is no narrative to speak of, no development, no outcome to the painful series of misfits, misunderstandings, maladjustments, except in the end a lightening of the mood, a ray of hope, which stands in relation to the rest of the book as chocolate to castor-oil—something to take the taste out.

L. P. Hartley on *The Road Back* by Erich Maria Remarque in the *Week-end Review*, May 1931

It is hard to find any great value in Gustave Flaubert's *Trois Contes*, which is the title of his last volume. He is well known as the leader of the school of French realists, but he has another side, a sort of love for picturesque details which he apparently collects from wide reading about the past. [...] In the first of these tales, "Un Coeur Simple," he makes a study of a servant woman, but, after all, the reader cannot help asking himself whether it is not work misapplied. What Flaubert shows us is much more how observant a realist he himself is than the sort of a woman the old servant was. Insignificant details are crowded onto every page, but simply for their own sake; when they are all in the tale ends, and the reader is left to admire or not to care for, as his nature may direct, a rather cold-blooded study of an ignorant, kindly old woman [...]. The last sketch, "Herodias," shows this quality even more strongly. It is crammed with the most motley and confused details, and reads like the dream of an opium-eater after it has been put into shape for publication, with the missing links ingeniously supplied.

Review of *Trois Contes* ("Three Tales") by Gustave Flaubert,
in *The Atlantic Monthly*, Vol. 40, 1877

Loveday—would you mind if I referred to her simply as L? I have my health to think of—is one of those cute, cute, cute, reckless, scatter-brained, daring, but golden-hearted, young women that always make me want to get out the trusty old gun that Grandpa carried all through the Civil War without firing a shot. Oh, how gaily and irresponsibly she does rattle on, all during the book! "Happy Me!" she calls herself, and she addresses her mother as "Lamb-bird." Then she has a little way of saying "quee" instead of "queer," and there is one occasion when she employs "pew" rather than use the less whimsical "pure." In short, I cannot tell you how not hungry it makes me to follow her conversation. "Debonair" may be her lover's word for her, but "God-awful" will ever be her nickname with me.

There is unfortunately so very much of L. in the book—and it's quee how little of that pew young thing is enough to last you a lifetime…

Dorothy Parker on the novel *Debonair* by G. B. Stern in
The New Yorker, April 1928

Why, Sir, if you were to read Richardson for the story, your impatience would be so much fretted that you would hang yourself.
Samuel Johnson on Samuel Richardson

The question now to be asked is whether Mrs. Wharton, with her undeniable skill and power and tact, has won us to her affirmative. Our reply is, No. For, taking away the pomp and circumstance, the argument amounts to this, that the powers of life and death should be vested in a nurse-girl. We have the highest admiration for the modern highly educated, well-trained nurse, and regard her as a very high product of civilisation; but, at her best, her business is to carry out the directions of her superiors, the medical men.

Country Life on *The Fruit of the Tree* by Edith Wharton, 1907

Why do they insist on discussing *Swann's Way* as a stage in the history of the novel? Is it a novel? Does it have any characters constructed in depth, or only figures used to exemplify metaphysical principles? Does it have a plot? You answer, "Look at this philistine, who thinks that a novel is supposed to have characters and a plot!" […]

You have to have Proust in your course, since everyone else has him in his, but instead of trying to prove his influence on ???, how about discussing him among the inbred and enfeebled descendants of Baudelaire?

Good-Books-Bad-Books.com's verdict on Marcel Proust's *Swann's Way (In Search of Lost Time, Vol 1)*

For this book, he [Benito Mussolini] thought up the title, Claudia Particella, L'Amante del Cardinale: Grande Romanzo dei Tempi del Cardinale Emanuel Madruzzo. Well do I know, from reading the newspapers, that those who attempt disagreement with the Dictator trifle with their health; so I shall but remark, in a quiet way, that if *The Cardinal's Mistress* is a grande romanzo, I am Alexandre Dumas, père et fils.

Dorothy Parker on *The Cardinal's Mistress* by Benito Mussolini in *The New Yorker*, September 1928

Bryson claims that "Yid" is an abbreviation of "Yiddish speaker,"
and his table comparing country-names in English to the native
forms is just plain dishonest. I also don't see why we should all
have to suffer because he can't distinguish between the meanings
of "swimming" as a gerund and "swimming" as a participle.

Good-Books-Bad-Books.com on Bill Bryson's
The Mother Tongue: English and How It Got That Way.

❧

The triumph of sugar over diabetes.

George Jean Nathan on J. M. Barrie

❧

He has driven some susceptible persons to crime in a very fury
of boredom.

Ezra Pound on the Romantic poet William Wordsworth

❧

The gentleman who taught me jewelry-making pointed out the
importance of the artist's manifest intention in an artwork: "If you
want to leave the visible part oxidized and dirty-looking, make sure
that the back sparkles." This is especially important in surrealist
works, where the line between form and anti-form is a little prob-
lematic to begin with. […] I have never read such a powerful novel
that produced so few visual images. The young prophetess clothed in
butterflies could have been stunning. In the end I had to build her
myself, and can't quite manage to finish her. Again, that might have
been fine, if it had been clear that Rushdie meant it that way. It isn't.
Who and what is the book about? Émigrés? Choice? The Creation?
The Satanic Verses left me confused and very depressed. And I'm not
at all sure that Rushdie meant it that way.

Good-Books-Bad-Books.com on
Salman Rushdie's *The Satanic Verses*

This obscure, eccentric, and disgusting poem.

Voltaire on John Milton's epic poem *Paradise Lost*

Theodore Dreiser
Should ought to write nicer.

Dorothy Parker reviewing *Dawn* by Dreiser
in *The New Yorker*, May 1931

What a bore! She's full of sentences like—writing of herself—
"She realizes that in English literature in her time she is the only
one. She has always known it and now she says it." This was in the
days of Shaw and Eliot. (You're the one who asked about Joyce,
not me.)

Miss Stein sometimes takes time out from praising Miss Stein
to drop names. Vast quantities of names. It's name-dropping
because she rarely has anything worthwhile to say about the people attached to them, although they were often the people who
did make a difference.

Good-Books-Bad-Books.com on Gertrude Stein's
The Autobiography of Alice B. Toklas

His writing, as he might have said himself, is like lace; the material is of very little consequence, the embroidery is all that counts;
and it shares with lace the happy faculty of coming out sometimes
in yards and yards.

Lytton Strachey on Horace Walpole

Paradise Lost is one of the books which the reader admires and lays down, and forgets to take up again. Its perusal is a duty rather than a pleasure.

Dr. Samuel Johnson on John Milton's epic poem

Why bother adding a few words to the swamp which has grown up around Beckett? Sometimes it's a good idea just to repeat what's simple and true, in the hope that somebody's listening.

I was recently forced by circumstances to re-read *Waiting for Godot*. I was bored sick. I haven't said that the work is inherently boring, and therefore there's no point in arguing with me unless you were there and saw that I wasn't bored sick. And it's not going to help much to say that its ennuiogenicity is part of the theme of the play. Pain is pain, boredom is boredom, and both have grave disadvantages even as artistic devices. […] Don't think that Beckett was pulling the critics' and the public's legs. Beckett had been playing Beckett so long that he believed it himself.

Good-Books-Bad-Books.com on Samuel Beckett's play
Waiting for Godot

Indeed the whole of Milton's poem, *Paradise Lost*, is such barbarous trash, so outrageously offensive to reason and to common sense that one is naturally led to wonder how it can have been tolerated by a people, amongst whom astronomy, navigation, and chemistry are understood.

William Cobbett on *Paradise Lost* in *A Year's Residence in the United States*, 1800

A monster gibbering shrieks, and gnashing imprecations against mankind—tearing down all shreds of modesty, past all sense of

manliness and shame; filthy in word, filthy in thought, furious, rag-
ing, obscene.

William Makepeace Thackeray on Jonathan Swift, author of
Gulliver's Travels

❧

Why, Sir, Sherry is dull, naturally dull; but it must have taken him
a great deal of pains to become what we now see him. Such
excess of stupidity, Sir, is not in nature.

Dr. Samuel Johnson on Thomas Sheridan

❧

They have no life outside the married state; their natures cannot
be fulfilled except in love; and they are always looking what love
they have in the mouth, so to speak, and bewailing the fact that it
has grown long in the tooth.

They are under-vitalised, I suppose. The story, whose end the
jacket discloses, is not a very gripping one.

L. P. Hartley on *A Note in Music* by Rosamund Lehmann in the
Week-end Review, August 1930

❧

They inculcate the morals of a whore, and the manners of a
dancing master.

Samuel Johnson on the publication of Lord Chesterfield's
letters of advice to his son, in James Boswell,
Life of Samuel Johnson, 1791

❧

Our language sank under him.

Joseph Addison on the poet John Milton

What would you have me retract? I thought your book an imposture; I think it an imposture still. For this opinion I have given my reasons to the publick which I here dare you to refute. Your rage I defy. Your abilities… are not so formidable; and what I hear of your morals, inclines me to pay regard not to what you shall say, but to what you shall prove. You may print this if you will.

Samuel Johnson in a letter to Mr. James MacPherson, the author of *Ossian* – a "translation" of an obscure Scottish epic poem which Johnson thought a forgery.

That he could not reason, that he had no wit, no humour, no eloquence, is apparent from his writings. Nature had made him a slave and an idolater. His mind resembled those creepers which the botanists call parasites and which can subsist only by clinging round the stems and imbibing the juices of stronger plants. Servile and impertinent, shallow and pedantic, a bigot and a sot, bloated with family pride, and eternally blustering about the dignity of a born gentleman, yet stooping to be a talebearer, a common butt in the taverns of London… Everything which another man would have hidden, everything the publication of which would have made another man hang himself, was matter of exaltation to his…diseased mind.

Thomas Babington Macaulay on James Boswell, the chronicler of Dr. Samuel Johnson

English literature's performing flea.

Sean O'Casey on P. G. Wodehouse

Had they wanted to, a number of people might have written Wonder Hero. (An American would probably have written it

best.)…Mr. Priestley's blunt pencil no doubt suffers from the contrast with Miss Ivy Compton Burnett's pointed pen. But I doubt if any stable companion would have done him much good. There is nothing worse than a "readable" book which you find difficulty in reading. (I, being a conscientious reviewer and a bad skipper, read every word.) Mr. Priestley has always been good at making a short story long. This is a short book.

Elizabeth Bibesco on *Wonder Hero* by J. P. Priestley
in the *Week-end Review*, September 1933

Here are Jonny Keats' piss-a-bed poetry, and three novels by God knows whom… No more Keats, I entreat: flay him alive; if some of you don't I must skin him myself: there is no bearing the drivelling idiotism of the Mankin.

Lord Byron on the Romantic poet John Keats

Our opinion then is this: that Barère approached nearer than any person mentioned in history or fiction, whether man or devil, to the idea of consummate and universal depravity. In him the qualities which are the proper objects of contempt, preserve an exquisite and absolute harmony. When we put everything together, sensuality, poltroonery, baseness, effrontery, mendacity, barbarity, the result is something which in a novel we should condemn as caricature, and to which, we venture to say, no parallel can be found in history… A man who has never been within the tropics does not know what a thunderstorm means; a man who has never looked on Niagara has but a faint idea of a cataract; and he who has not read Barère's Memoirs may be said not to know what it is to lie.

Thomas Babington Macaulay on Bertrand Barère
de Vieuzac's *Mémoires*

"The Phrenzy of the Poems" was bad enough in its way; but it did not alarm us half so seriously as the calm, settled, imperturbable drivelling idiocy of Endymion…Mr. Hunt is a small poet, but he is a clever man. Mr. Keats is a still smaller poet, and he is only a boy of pretty abilities, which he has done everything in his power to spoil…We venture to make one small prophecy, that his bookseller will not a second time venture £50 upon any thing he can write.

Blackwood's Magazine on *Endymion* by John Keats, 1818

Persons attempting to find a motive in this narrative will be prosecuted; persons attempting to find a moral in it will be banished; persons attempting to find a plot in it will be shot.

Mark Twain

Fricassee of dead dog…A truly unwise little book. The kind of man that Keats was gets ever more horrible to me. Force of hunger for pleasure of every kind, and want of all other force— such a soul, it would once have been very evident, was a chosen "vessel of Hell."

Thomas Carlyle on Monkton Milnes's
Life and Letters of Keats, 1848

Mr. Shelley is a very vain man; and like most vain men, he is but half instructed in knowledge and less than half disciplined in reasoning powers; his vanity… has been his ruin.

Quarterly Review on Percy Bysshe Shelley, 1817

The same old sausage, fizzing and sputtering in its own grease.
Henry James on Thomas Carlyle

At bottom, this Macaulay is but a poor creature with his dictionary literature and erudition, his saloon arrogance. He has no
vision in him. He will neither see nor do anything great.
Thomas Carlyle on Thomas Babington Macaulay

Shelley is a poor creature, who has said or done nothing worth a
serious man being at the trouble of remembering... Poor soul, he
has always seemed to me an extremely weak creature; a poor,
thin, spasmodic, hectic, shrill, and pallid being... The very voice of
him, shrill, shrieky, to my ear has too much of the ghost.
Thomas Carlyle on the Romantic poet Percy Bysshe Shelley

Walt Whitman is as unacquainted with art as a hog
with mathematics.
Anonymous critic in the *London Critic*

As to Mr. Shelley's virtues, if he belonged (as we understand he
did), to a junta, whose writings tend to make our sons profligates,
and our daughters strumpets, we ought justly to regret the
decease of the Devil (if that were possible), as one of his coadju-
tors. Seriously speaking, however, we feel no pleasure in the

untimely death of this Tyro of the Juan school, that pre-eminent Academy of Infidels, Blasphemers, Seducers, and Wantons. We had much rather have heard, that he had been consigned to a Monastery of La Trappe, for correction of their dangerous principles, and expurgation of their corrupt minds.

Gentleman's Magazine on the Romantic poet
Percy Bysshe Shelley, 1822

Is Wordsworth a bell with a wooden tongue?
Ralph Waldo Emmerson

The Vivien of Mr. Tennyson's idyll seems to me…about the most base and repulsive person ever set forth in serious literature. Her impurity is actually eclipsed by her incredible and incomparable vulgarity…She is such a sordid creature as plucks men passing by the sleeve.

Algernon Swinburne on Alfred, Lord Tennyson

A weak, diffusive, weltering, ineffectual man. … Never did I see such apparatus got ready for thinking, and so little thought. He mounts scaffolding, pulleys, and tackle, gathers all the tools in the neighbourhood with labour, with noise, demonstration, precept, abuse, and sets—three bricks.

Thomas Carlyle on Romantic poet
Samuel Taylor Coleridge

I attempt to describe Mr. Swinburne; and lo! the Bacchanal screams, the sterile Dolores sweats, serpents dance, men and women wrench, wriggle, and foam in an endless alliteration of heated and meaningless words.

Robert Buchanan on the poet Algernon Swinburne

A lewd vegetarian.

Charles Kingsley passing judgement on Percy Bysshe Shelley

Of all the writers we have perused, Walt Whitman is the most silly, the most blasphemous, and the most disgusting.

Literary Gazette, 1860

If the author's object was to realize an American bore so perfectly that most of his readers would feel as if they were suffering from the man himself, he may be congratulated on a masterly performance.

The English Review, July 1928, on
The Man who knew Coolidge by Sinclair Lewis

I could readily see in Emerson...a gaping flaw. It was the insinuation that had he lived in those days when the world was made, he might have offered some valuable suggestions.

Herman Melville on Ralph Waldo Emerson.

Emerson's writing has a cold, cheerless glitter, like the new furniture in a warehouse, which will come of use by and by.

Alexander Smith on Ralph Waldo Emerson,
Dreamthorp, 1864

The back cover suggests that it can be read as a guide to "upper-class" life. But this is misleading. As the text itself makes clear, Henry and Caroline are not, and are not about to become, either owners or controllers of any significant proportion of the means of production. Sloane Rangers are the subalterns and field officers, not the major-generals commanding, of the fortress heights of the economy and the state. They are not the rapacious financiers or the galvanic industrialists or the power-hungry politicos. Henry's job in the City or the wine trade and Caroline's little Trust can keep them safely afloat at the level of public school fees, a (Dreaded) Au Pair, Supertravel skiing holidays, Hermes scarves, General Trading Company ice-buckets, engraved writing paper, hunt bollock tickets, teeny silver thimbles for the dowyrette, and the Volvo Estate car with bars for the Labrador. But it's Blanquette de Limeaux, not Moët, in the Buck's Fizz...

W. G. Runciman on *The Sloane Ranger's Handbook: The First Guide to What Really Matters in Life* by Ann Barr and Peter York, in the *London Review of Books*, 1982

I have difficulty in describing...the character of Mr. Joyce's morality...he is a literary charlatan of the extremest order. His principal book, Ulysses...is an anarchical production, infamous in taste, in style, in everything...He is a sort of M. de Sade, but does not write so well.

Edmund Gosse on James Joyce

Under the dirty clumsy paws of a harper whose plectrum is a muck-rake, any tune will become a chaos of dischords. ...Mr. Whitman's Eve is a drunken apple-woman, indecently sprawling in the slush and garbage of the gutter amid the rotten refuse of her overturned fruit-stall: but Mr. Whitman's Venus is a Hottentot wench under the influence of cantharides and adulterated rum.

Algernon Swinburne on Walt Whitman

The best answer to his twaddle is cui bono?—a very little Latin phrase very generally mistranslated and misunderstood—cui bono? to whom is it a benefit? If not to Mr. Emerson individually, then surely to no man.

Edgar Allan Poe on Ralph Waldo Emerson,
Autobiography, 1842

Bernard Shaw is an excellent man; he has not an enemy in the world, and none of his friends like him.

Oscar Wilde

What is Conrad but the wreck of Stevenson floating about in the slipsop of Henry James.

George Moore on the novelist Joseph Conrad

There are two ways of disliking poetry: one way is to dislike it, the other is to read Pope.

Oscar Wilde

I am not an editor of a newspaper and shall always try to do right
and be good so that God will not make me one.

Mark Twain

What does pain me exceedingly is that you should write so badly.
These verses are execrable, and I am shocked that you seem
unable to perceive it.

Edmund Gosse to Robert Nichols

The first 200 pages of *Ulysses*…Never have I read such tosh. As
for the first two chapters we will let them pass, but the 3rd, 4th
5th, 6th—merely the scratchings of pimples on the body of the
bootboy at Claridges.

Virginia Woolf on James Joyce in a letter to
Lytton Strachey, 24 April 1922

The last part of it is the dirtiest, most indecent, most obscene
thing ever written. Yes it is, Frieda… it is filthy.

D. H. Lawrence on James Joyce's *Ulysses*

A combination of Little Nell and Lady Macbeth.

Alexander Woollcott on Dorothy Parker
in *While Rome Burns*

Trollope! Did anyone bear a name that predicted a style more Trollopy?

George Moore on Anthony Trollope

❀

This is not a novel to be tossed aside lightly. It should be thrown with great force.

Dorothy Parker

❀

Very nice, though there are dull stretches.

Antoine de Rivarol on a two-line poem

❀

Your manuscript is both good and original; but the part that is good is not original, and the part that is original is not good.

Samuel Johnson to an anonymous writer

❀

The more I read him, the less I wonder that they poisoned him.

Thomas Babington Macaulay on Socrates

❀

The author has great cleverness, or rather he has a great deal of small cleverness. In great cleverness there must be an element of honest wisdom, we like to imagine, such as *Lothair* is fatally without. Still, he has cleverness enough to elicit repeatedly the reader's applause. A certain cleverness is required for getting into difficulties, for creating them and causing them to bristle around you; and of this peril-seeking faculty Mr. Disraeli possesses an abundant measure. Out of his difficulties he never emerges, so that in the end his talent lies gloriously entombed and enshrined in a vast edifice of accumulated mistakes.

> **Review** of *Lothair* by Benjamin Disraeli,
> in *The Atlantic Monthly*, Vol. 26, 1870

Take from him his sophisms, futilities, and incomprehensibilities and what remains? His foggy mind.

> **Thomas Jefferson** on Plato

I am reading Proust for the first time. Very poor stuff. I think he was mentally defective.

> **Evelyn Waugh** on French writer Marcel Proust, in a letter to
> John Betjeman, 1948. From *The Letters of Evelyn Waugh* (1980)

The language of Aristophanes reeks of his miserable quackery: it is made up of the lowest and most miserable puns; he doesn't even please the people, and to men of judgment and honor he is intolerable; his arrogance is insufferable, and all honest men detest his malice.

> **Plutarch** on Aristophanes (c.440–c.380 BC), Greek playwright

The most vulgar-minded genius that ever produced a great effect in literature.

> **George Eliot** on Lord Byron in a letter
> dated 21 September 1869

Jane Austen's books, too, are absent from this library. Just that one omission alone would make a fairly good library out of a library that hadn't a book in it.

Mark Twain on Jane Austen

I have received your new book against the human race. I thank you for it. You will please mankind to whom you tell a few home truths but you will not correct it. You depict with very true colors the horrors of human society which out of ignorance and weakness sets its hopes on so many comforts. Never has so much wit been used in an attempt to make us like animals. The desire to walk on all fours seizes one when one reads your work.

Voltaire, in a letter to Jean-Jacques Rousseau, 1755, after reading Rousseau's *Discourse on the Origin of Inequality among Men*, which praised primitive man over his "civilized" neighbors

George Moore wrote brilliant English until he discovered grammar.

Oscar Wilde

I am at a loss to understand why people hold Miss Austen's novels at so high a rate, which seem to me vulgar in tone, sterile in artistic invention, imprisoned in the wretched conventions of English society, without genius, wit, or knowledge of the world. Never was life so pinched and narrow. The one problem in the mind of the writer in both the stories I have read...is marriage-bleness. All that interests in any character introduced is still this one—Has he or (she) the money to marry with and conditions conforming? 'Tis the "nympholepsy of a fond despair," say, rather, of an English boarding-house. Suicide is more respectable.

Ralph Waldo Emerson on Jane Austen, *Journal*, 1861

I wish her characters would talk a little less like the heroes and heroines of police reports.

George Eliot on the novel *Jane Eyre* by Charlotte Brontë

His versification is so destitute of sustained harmony, many of his thoughts are so strained, his sentiments so unamiable, his misanthropy so gloomy, his libertinism so shameless, his merriment such a grinning of a ghastly smile, that I have always believed his verses would soon rank with forgotten things.

John Quincy Adams on the poetry of Lord Byron in his *Memoirs*, 1830

Truman Capote has made lying an art. A minor art.

Gore Vidal

I like a thin book because it will steady a table, a leather volume because it will strop a razor, and a heavy book because it can be thrown at a cat.

Mark Twain

Of Dickens's style it is impossible to speak in praise. It is jerky, ungrammatical, and created by himself in defiance of rules…No young novelist should ever dare to imitate the style of Dickens.

Anthony Trollope on Charles Dickens, in his *Autobiography*, 1883

I found out in the first two pages that it was a woman's writing— she supposed that in making a door, you last of all put in the panels!

Thomas Caryle on *Adam Bede* by George Eliot

Every great man nowadays has his disciples, and it is always Judas who writes the biography.

Oscar Wilde

All the faults of *Jane Eyre* are magnified a thousandfold, and the only consolation which we have in reflecting upon it is that it will never be generally read.

James Lorrimer, a contemporary critic, on Emily Brontë's novel *Wuthering Heights* in the *North British Review*

I have just read *Dombey and Son*. The worst book in the world.

Evelyn Waugh on Dickens' novel, in a letter to Laura Waugh, 23 January 1945. From *The Letters of Evelyn Waugh* (1980)

The general theory of life on which [*The Pickwick Papers*] is based is not only false, but puerile. Fifty years hence most of his wit will be harder to understand than the allusions in the Dunciad; and our grandchildren will wonder what their ancestors could have meant by putting Mr. Dickens at the head of the novelists of his day.

James Stephens in the *Saturday Review*, 1858

A hack writer who would not have been considered fourth rate in Europe, who tried out a few of the old proven "sure-fire" literary skeletons with sufficient local color to intrigue the superficial and the lazy.

William Faulkner on Mark Twain

Conrad spent a day finding the *mot juste* and then killed it.

Ford Madox Ford on Joseph Conrad

He is a man with a very active fancy, great powers of language, much perception of what is grotesque, and a most lachrymose and melodramatic turn of mind—and this is all. He has never played any significant part in any movement than that of a fly… on a wheel.

Saturday Review on Charles Dickens, 1857

Lady Chatterley's Lover—Mr. Lawrence has a diseased mind. He is obsessed by sex and we have no doubt that he will be ostracised by all except the most degenerate coteries of the world.

John Bull magazine, 1928

It, the chef d'oeuvre of Madame Elinor Glyn, has come into my life. And Sherman's coming into Atlanta is but a sneaking, tiptoe performance in comparison.

> **Dorothy Parker** on a novel by the English author of sultry romances in *The New Yorker*, November 1927

As a writer he mastered everything except language; as a novelist he can do everything except tell a story; as an artist, everything except articulate.

> **Oscar Wilde** on George Meredith, British novelist and poet

…vain nashe, railing Nashe, cracking Nashe, bibbing Nashe, swaddish nashe…roguish nashe…the swish-swash of the press, the bum of impudency, the shambles of beastliness…the toadstool of the realm.

> **Gabriel Harvey** on the English playwright Thomas Nashe

Whether Kallman was the wrong blond is the whole question of it. The right blond, Miller, would also have been the wrong blond, so maybe the wrong blond was the right one, wrong blond(e)s after all having some tradition in literature: Lord Alfred Douglas, Zelda Fitzgerald, Marilyn Monroe, to name but three who were all wrong, all right. This account of the relationship between Auden and Kallman is written by the blond's late-in-the-day stepmother, Dorothy J. Farnan, also blond, who, if not wrong, is not always right, but very readable for all that.

> **Alan Bennett** on Dorothy Farnan's biography of Auden, *Auden in Love*, in the *London Review of Books*, 1985

I have no patience with the sort of trash you send me out by way of books...I never saw such work or works. Campbell is lecturing, Moore idling, Southey twaddling, Wordsworth drivelling, Coleridge muddling, Joanna Baillie piddling, Bowles quibbling, squabbling, and snivelling.

Lord Byron on the Romantic Poets

Monsieur Zola is determined to show that if he has not genius he can at least be dull.

Oscar Wilde on the French novelist Émile Zola

Mr. Southey wades through ponderous volumes of travels and old chronicles, from which he carefully selects all that is false, useless and absurd, as being essentially poetical; and when he has a commonplace book full of monstrosities, strings them into an epic.

Thomas Love Peacock on the British poet laureate Robert Southey, in *The Four Ages of Poetry*, 1820

This dodipoule, this didpopper...why, thou arrant butter whoe, thou coteueane & scrattop of scoldes, will thou never leave affecting a dead Carcasse...a wispe, a wispe, rippe, rippe, you kitchen-stuff wrangler!

Thomas Nashe, a 16th-century pamphleteer, on Gabriel Harvey

I have a theory about the modern Teddy-boy school of novelist & critic—[John] Wain, [Kingsley] Ames [sic] etc. It is that they all

read English Literature for schools and so take against it, while good critics & writers read as a treat and a relaxation from Latin & Greek.

  Evelyn Waugh in a letter to Christopher Sykes, 15 July 1955.
From *The Letters of Evelyn Waugh* (1980)

… he is the dullest Briton of them all.

  Henry James on Anthony Trollope, in a letter, 1 November 1875

I am reading *Chartreuse de Parme* (in translation) for the first time. Why is it called the first "psychological" novel? It seems to me that nothing any character thinks or says or does has any relation to human nature as I know it.

  Evelyn Waugh in a letter to Ann Fleming, 17 June 1957.
From *The Letters of Evelyn Waugh* (1980)

This awful Whitman. This post-mortem poet. This poet with the private soul leaking out of him all the time.

  D. H. Lawrence on Walt Whitman,
Studies in Classic American Literature, 1923

Her works will be read with disgust by every female who has any pretensions to delicacy; with detestation by everyone attached to the interests of religion and morality, and with indignation by anyone who might feel any regard for the unhappy woman whose frailties should have been buried in oblivion.

  Anonymous, on Mary Wollstonecraft,
in the *Historical Magazine*, 1799

Her latest novel, *The Sweetest Dream*, is the biggest hodgepodge of styles, themes, and characters yet: a novel whose moments of brilliance are obscured by reams of tiresome exposition, hokey plot twists, and astonishingly opaque characters... The reader is left with the sense that Ms. Lessing is simply tossing everything she's ever written about before into this kitchen sink of a novel, with no regard to the niceties of narrative construction or rudiments of storytelling...and while Ms. Lessing succeeds in showing us the hypocrisy of these parlor-room Communists, her efforts are so heavy-handed and long-winded that she nearly puts us to sleep in the process.

Michiko Kakutani on *The Sweetest Dream* by Doris Lessing
in *The New York Times*, 1 February 2002

I really think that three-quarters of it [her poetry] is gibberish. However, I must crush down these thoughts, otherwise the dove of peace will shit on me.

Nöel Coward on Dame Edith Sitwell

Mrs. Baker's style has a deliberately offhand, tomboy quality, which under its surface swagger, is soft, blurred, and rather sloppy. Her indistinct, often careless, sometimes ungrammatical sentences show a disregard for accuracy and clarity in the interest of manner and mannerism. She seems to give a kind of imitation of simplicity. Instead of being disarmed, the reader is likely to arm at once.

Eudora Welty on *Our Gifted Son* by Dorothy Baker,
reviewed in *The New York Times Book Review*, 15 August 1948.
Reprinted in *A Writer's Eye* (1994)

Here is Miss Seward with six tomes of the most disgusting trash, sailing over the Styx with a Foolscap over her periwig as complacent as can be—Of all Bitches dead or alive a scribbling woman is the most canine.

Lord Byron on Anna Seward

The only kind of reader likely to persevere with *The Runaway Soul* is the one who fears he may not be intelligent enough to grasp the author's meaning. After years of gestation, this is his first novel, and the publisher's blurb describes it as having been "eagerly awaited." By whom, for heaven's sake?

Charles Osborne on a novel by Harold Brodkey, in the *Jewish Chronicle*, 21 February 1992

Books that have become classics—books that have had their day and now get more praise than perusal—always remind me of retired colonels and majors and captains who, having reached the age limit, find themselves retired on half-pay.

Thomas Bailey Aldrich

The reason why so few good books are written is that so few people who can write know anything.

Walter Bagehot

Circumlocution, n. A literary trick whereby the writer who has nothing to say breaks it gently to the reader.

Ambrose Bierce

…if those only wrote, who were sure of being read, we should have fewer authors; and the shelves of libraries would not groan beneath the weight of dusty tomes more voluminous than luminous.

Marguerite Blessington

A big book is a big nuisance.

Callimachus, third century BC; also quoted as "Big book, big evil"

I think you must remember that a writer is a simple-minded person to begin with and go on that basis.

Erskine Caldwell

A very good library could be started by leaving Jane Austen out.

Mark Twain

I never read any novels except my own. When I feel worried, agitated or upset, I read one and find the last pages soothe me and leave me happy. I quite understand why I am popular in hospitals.

Barbara Cartland

He is not really a writer, but a non-stop talker to whom some-one has given a typewriter.

Gerald Brenan, referring to Henry Miller. *Thoughts in a Dry Season* (1978)

Most contemporary books give the impression of having been manufactured in a day, out of books read the day before.
Sebastian-Roch-Nicolas Chamfort

Thank you for the manuscript; I shall lose no time in reading it.
Benjamin Disraeli's stock reply to authors who sent him unsolicited copies of their works (attrib.)

In one place in *The Deerslayer*, and in the restricted space of two-thirds of a page, Cooper has scored 114 offences against literary art out of a possible 115. It breaks the record.
Mark Twain

I couldn't write the things they publish now, with no beginning and no end, and a little incest in the middle.
Irvin S. Cobb

Mr. Oscar Wilde is no poet, but a cleverish man who has an infinite contempt for his readers, and thinks he can take them in with a little mouthing verse.
Anonymous review in the *Spectator*, 13 August 1881

The greatest masterpiece in literature is only a dictionary out of order.
Jean Cocteau

Madame Bovary is the sexiest book imaginable. The woman's virtually a nymphomaniac but you won't find a vulgar word in the entire thing.

Noel Coward

It is one of the misfortunes of life that one must read thousands of books only to discover that one need not have read them.

Thomas de Quincey

What is responsible for the success of many works is the rapport between the mediocrity of the author's ideas and the mediocrity of the public's.

Sebastian-Roch-Nicolas Chamfort

There are books of which the backs and covers are by far the best parts.

Charles Dickens

She guanoed her mind by reading French novels.

Benjamin Disraeli

I enjoy reading biographies because I want to know about the people who messed up the world.

Marie Dressler

The first thing to have in a libry is a shelf. Fr'm time to time this can be decorated with lithrachure. But th' shelf is th' main thing.
Finley Peter Dunne

To invent good stories, and to tell them well, are possibly very rare talents, and yet I have observed few persons who have scrupled to aim at both.
Henry Fielding

A story with a moral appended is like the bite of a mosquito. It bores you, and then injects a stinging drop to irritate your conscience.
O. Henry

A book on cheap paper does not convince. It is not prized, it is like a wheezy doctor with pigtail tobacco breath, who needs a manicure.
Elbert Hubbard

Currently, there are two kinds of serious-novel. The first deals with the Human Condition (often confused, in Manhattan, with marriage) while the second is a word-structure that deals only with itself. Although the Human Condition novel can be read—if not fully appreciated—by any moderately competent reader of the late Dame Agatha Christie, the second cannot be read at all. The word-structure novel is intended to be taught, rather like a gnostic text whose secrets may only be revealed by tenured adepts in sunless campus chapels.
Gore Vidal in his review of Doris Lessing's novel *Shikasta*, in *The New York Review of Books*, 20 December 1979

He is, indeed, the most formidable personality among that turbulent militia of young writers who march behind Mr. Hemingway in his campaign for literary low-living and plain speaking. Everybody and everything Mr. Faulkner writers about is low and rabid. Rape and murder are as common in his books as flirtation and disagreement in others: his genius is drawn, as the moth to the star, to secret knifings and the bursting of gas bombs. [...] Mr. Faulkner does what he sets out to do wonderfully well... But he never leaves us wholly convinced that what he does is worth doing.

L. P. Hartley on *These Thirteen* by William Faulkner in the
Week-end Review, September 1933

It was a book to kill time for those who liked it better dead.
Rose Macaulay

American Novel: A story in which two people want each other from the beginning but don't get each other until the end of the book.
French Novel: A story in which the two people get together right at the beginning, but from then until the end of the book they don't want each other any more.
Russian Novel: A story in which the two people don't want each other or get each other—and for 800 pages brood about it.

Erich Maria Remarque

Novelists might be the greatest possible help to us if they painted life as it is, and human feelings in their true proportion and relaxation, but for the most part they have been and are altogether noxious.

William Dean Howells

mistaken for an anchor-chain running out from the adjoining yacht, and wearing gamboge shoes. To England, by representing its upper classes as degenerate to an Hon., and its lower barely able to utter "R" and spit at a passing dog. To publishers, for describing one of them as a fat, double-chinned, pot-bellied son of Belial with pig's eyes and a licentious look, and for giving him the name Mortimer, well known among Wodehouse students as his black accolade of scorn. And, perhaps above all, to Love. He has degraded both the tender passion and its language. "He stared at her like a bear at a bun." Is this any way to capture the miracle of love at first sight? (Cf. Romeo and Juliet, II, i.)

J. B. Boothroyd on P. G. Wodehouse in *Punch*, 1 August 1956

I have always had the greatest contempt for novels written with a purpose.

Ford Madox Ford

I am only one, only one, only one. Only one being, one at the same time. Not two, not three, only one. Only one life to live, only sixty minutes in one hour. Only one pair of eyes. Only one brain. Only one being. Being only one, having only one pair of eyes, having only one time, having only one life, I cannot read your MS three or four times. Not even one time. Only one look, only one look is enough. Hardly one copy would sell here. Hardly one. Hardly one. Many thanks. I am returning the MS by registered post. Only one Ms by one post.

Rejection letter from the editor **A. J. Fifield** to Gertrude Stein, who was renowned for her repetitive literary style

Perhaps Vonnegut feels in his aching bones that a new Nineteen-hundred and Twenty-nine will soon wreck the economy, or perhaps the book simply slips from his grasp; but whatever the explanation, the final chapters are a shambles.

James Wolcott on *Jailbird* by Kurt Vonnegut,
in *The New York Review of Books,* 22 November 1979

Whenever the literary German dives into a sentence, that is the last you are going to see of him till he emerges on the other side of his Atlantic with his verb in his mouth.

Mark Twain

The fact that the *Odyssey* is the "oldest book worth reading for its story and the first novel of modern Europe" makes it no more lively—to me, anyway—than does the turning of it into what Mr. Shaw's publishers call "vital, modern, poetic prose." The menaces in ancient Jeopardy were far too apart...the gods maundered and were repetitious. *Ulysses* himself is not a hero to whom a young man's fancy turns in any season...The brazen entry into the United States of Mr. Joyce's *Ulysses* has most recently brought the *Odyssey* again into view; as the magazine *Time* points out to its surprised readers, "almost every detail of the *Odyssey's* action can be found in disguised form in *Ulysses.*" So, many a reader might naturally enough ask, what? So nothing— that is, nothing of real importance in so far as the *Odyssey* or *Ulysses* itself is concerned. The ancient story just happened to make a point of departure for Mr. Joyce. He might equally have taken for a pattern Sherman's campaign in Georgia.

James Thurber on the *Odyssey of Homer*, in *The Odyssey of Disney*, first published in *The Nation*, 28 March 1934.
Reprinted in *Collecting Himself*, ed. Michael J. Rosen
(Hamish Hamilton, 1989)

A provincial manufacturer of gauche and heavy fictions that sometimes have corresponding values.

F. R. Leavis on Thomas Hardy

If he had ever devoted half as much time and intelligence, say, to the study of Christian teachings, as Catholics have to the study of his opinions, he would be by now either a Roman Catholic or a reprobate. As it is, he is neither. He is Bernard Shaw, a man driven, as under the lash of the furies, by a passionate intellectual intolerance which makes all his great gifts futile.

W. T. Kane on George Bernard Shaw
in *The Month*, no. 758, August 1927

Miss Mannin made her journey to Russia to discover the New Commonwealth. It was not as clean as she expected, and she wisely decided that she prefers cleanliness to Left-Wing progress. A decision to be applauded.

The English Review volume 64, number 1, January 1937,
on *South to Samarkand* by Ethel Mannin

Here is a full-grown man, presumably intelligent and cultivated, putting on record for other full-grown men to read, the most secret mysteries of sexual connection, and that with so sickening a desire to reproduce the sensual mood, so careful a choice of epithet to convey mere animal sensations, that we merely shudder at the shameless nakedness.

The Contemporary Review, vol. 18, October 1871—
referring to Dante Gabriel Rossetti in an article entitled
"The Fleshly School of Poetry"

Unless the creations of an author's brain seize the attention and exercise the mind of his readers they are not worth considering at all; but a less amusing set of people never filled the imaginary world of a novelist than have been chosen for the pages of *The Secret Agent*...In fact, if Mr. Conrad was aiming at art and immortality instead of at filling up a definite number of pages, he could have reduced this story to a tenth part of its present dimensions, and still rather added to rather than taken away from its merits.

Country Life on Joseph Conrad, 21 September 1907.

We cannot sum up the merits of the stupendous mass of paper which lies before us, better than by saying, that it consists of about two thousand closely printed pages, that it occupies fifteen hundred inches cubic measure, and that it weighs sixty pounds avoirdupois.

Lord Macaulay on Edward Nare's three-volume
Memoirs of William Cecil, Lord Burghley in
the *Edinburgh Review*, April 1832

From the moment I picked up your book until I laid it down, I was convulsed with laughter. Some day I intend reading it.

Groucho Marx in the blurb written for S. J. Perelman's
1928 book *Dawn Ginsberg's Revenge*

Plato is a bore.

Friedrich Nietzsche

No, I didn't think *Lolita* any good except as smut. As that it was highly exciting to me.

Evelyn Waugh on Nabokov's novel *Lolita* in a letter to Nancy Mitford, 29 June 1959. From *The Letters of Evelyn Waugh* (1980)

This fictional account of the day-by-day life of an English gamekeeper is still of considerable interest to outdoor-minded readers, as it contains many passages on pheasant raising, the apprehending of poachers, ways to control vermin, and other chores and duties of the professional gamekeeper. Unfortunately one is obliged to wade through many passages of extraneous material in order to discover and savour these sidelights on the management of a Midlands shooting estate, and in this reviewer's opinion this book cannot take the place of J. R. Miller's *Practical Gamekeeping*.

Anonymous review of D. H. Lawrence's *Lady Chatterley's Lover*, attributed to Field and Stream, c. 1928.

Clearly, no expense, no drudgery of research and selection and compiling, were spared in the preparation of this volume. And now—to whom will it be a companion? The librarians, the collectors, the rare book dealers, the thesis writers—yes, all of these from now on. But hardly for the children. It is a reference book, but if a book concerns children, it should be theirs to consult.

Eudora Welty on *The Oxford Companion to Children's Literature* edited by Humphrey Carpenter and Mari Prichard, reviewed in *The New York Times Book Review*, 19 August 1984. Reprinted in *A Writer's Eye* (1994)

I think her lack of popularity is due to her habit of dissecting her bowels and displaying for public observation.

Maine Life on novelist May Sarton

Arnold is a dandy Isiah, a poet without passion, whose verse, written in a surplice, is for freshmen and for gentle maidens who will be wooed to the arms of these future rectors.

George Meredith in the *Fortnightly Review*, July 1909

The greatest of superficial novelists...It were, in our opinion, an offence against humanity to place Mr. Dickens among the greatest novelists.

Henry James

Her mind is a very thin soil, lain an inch or two upon very barren rock.

Virginia Woolf on Katherine Mansfield in
A Writer's Diary (1953), 7 August 1918

A great author, notwithstanding his Dictionary is imperfect, his Rambler pompous, his Idler inane, his Lives unjust, his poetry inconsiderable, his learning common, his ideas vulgar, his Irene a child of mediocrity, his genius worldly, his politics narrow, and his religion bigoted.

The critic **Robert Potter** on his contemporary Samuel Johnson

He writes like a sick man.

Gertrude Stein on D. H. Lawrence

A pair of boots is in every sense better than Pushkin…Pushkin is mere luxury and nonsense.

Fedor Dostoevsky, *Epokha*

People who like this sort of thing will find this the sort of thing they like.

Abraham Lincoln's review of a book

The covers of this book are too far apart.

Ambrose Bierce (attrib.)

The author, a young American novelist, is obviously a great admirer of Ernest Hemingway and James Joyce and D. H. Lawrence: his style and method continually pay homage to theirs. But his theme is one that might have recommended itself to the author of *The Rosary*, and I cannot help thinking that, all things considered, Mrs. Barclay would have made a better job of it, at any rate a more successful work of art.

L. P. Hartley on *Soldier's Pay* by William Faulkner
in the *Week-end Review*, July 1930

Howl is meant to be a noun, but I can't help taking it as an imperative.

John Hollander on *Howl* by Allen Ginsberg
in the *Partisan Review*

There are the old raptures about mountains and cataracts; the old flimsy philosophy about the effect of scenery upon the mind; the old crazy, mystical metaphysics; the endless wilderness of dull, flat, prosaic twaddle; and here and there fine descriptions and energetic declamations interspersed.

Thomas Babington Macaulay on the poet
William Wordsworth, journal entry, July 1850

So if you want a book that offers you everything, I highly suggest Mr. Webster's The Dictionary. I imagine there should be a Cliff Notes version of it out soon, which would contain only the words you need to know, which is always a good thing to own. Spread the word.

Tune in next week when I review...The Yellow Pages (just kidding).

Steven J. Willett of *Rant 'n' Rave* (www.rantrave.com) on
Webster's new Dictionary

Swine-born.

Punch on the Romantic poet Algernon Swinburne

What Centaur have we here, half man, half beast, neighing shrill defiance to all the world? What conglomerate of thought is this before us, with insolence, philosophy, tenderness, blasphemy, beauty, and gross indecency tumbling in drunken confusion through the pages? Who is this arrogant young man who proclaims himself the Poet of the Time, and who roots like a pig among a rotten garbage of licentious thoughts?

Walt Whitman attacked by the
New York Daily Times, 13 November 1856

I hate things all fiction…there should always be some foundation of fact for the most airy fabric and pure invention is but the talent of a liar.

Lord Byron in a letter to John Murray, 2 April 1817

The men, with one or two exceptions, are an unattractive lot, unkind and overbearing when in work, querulous and resentful when out of it, and ill-mannered always. Harry is a nice lad but rather colourless until his fellow apprentices undertake literally to paint him red—a shameful and disgusting scene. Certain injudicious reformers would no doubt excuse it with the parrot cry of degrading social conditions, but they would be wrong, for the incident could be paralleled at our great public schools, and is symptomatic of a baseness of fibre in the Anglo-Saxon race, more likely to be purged by prayer and fasting than by improved sanitation.

L. P. Hartley on *Love on the Dole* by Walter Greenwood
in the *Week-end Review*, July 1933

He describes London like a special correspondent for posterity.

Walter Bagehot on Charles Dickens
in the *National Review*, 7 October 1858

Cicero's style bores me. When I have spent an hour reading him —a good deal for me—and try to recollect what I have extracted, I usually find it nothing but wind.

Montaigne

Books bored me to death. I am disgusted with all that; only Victor Hugo's theatre and poetry and a book by Sainte-Beuve gave me any pleasure. I am absolutely fed up with literature.

Charles Baudelaire

The multitude of books is making us ignorant.

Voltaire

Television & Radio

In a recent instalment the magic animals formed an orchestra and their reported speech consisted of such expressions as "We are poised," said Brian, "Get your hooves out of it," "Ignore all harp cues," "Come on, Kitten-on-the-Keys," "Great Oaf!," "How humiliating!" "Prepared to give her all," "undaunted," "And lovely with it." Now I am prepared to believe that a number of retarded adults and professional puppeteers find this sort of whimsy deliciously sophisticated and deliciously funny, but I doubt whether it satisfies the nippers.

Bernard Hollowood on *The Magic Roundabout* in *Punch*,
26 January 1972

MTV makes me want to smoke crack...

Beck, 1992

Don't miss *Triangle* (BBC1), a thrilling new series about "life on an international passenger ferry." The international passenger ferry goes from Folkestone to Amsterdam...Look forward to innumerable future episodes of a series that does for international passenger ferries what Sink the Bismarck! did for the Bismarck.

Clive James in the *Observer*, 11 January 1981

Sure, there's a lot of information on the screen during any moment of CNN's new Headline News, but it changes so quickly you can't read it anyway.

Besides, if you did read half of those factoids, bullets, and graphics, they wouldn't make sense. Like this headline from Tuesday evening: "POTUS calling: Bush on holiday uses high tech means to talk to staff."

OK. That would be a cellphone?

This revamped, juiced-up Headline News—news at "the speed of life," they say—is 10 days old now, and you have to give CNN credit: It saved us all some time by taking a dull, useful news service and making it completely irrelevant.

Rick Kushman of the *Sacramento Bee*, 16 August 2001

Watching this programme, there are moments when you'd swear that Bob Dylan was actually dead, in so emphatically past tense is the story told, so respectful, indeed quietly monumental is its tone. The voice-over could almost be reciting his obituary from The Times. And then, almost at the last minute in the final section which telescopes the last two decades into a fifth of the running time, the mood suddenly switches as we are reassured that Bob, far from being busy dyin', is busy being reborn (and not for the first time).

Mat Snow on *Bob Dylan: The American Troubadour*,
for *Rock's Backpages*, March 2001

Secrets of the Guillotine (Channel 5) was a slow, painful way to spend 30 minutes. Which isn't to say I didn't learn anything, because I did. I learnt that the guillotine's blade travels two metres in three-quarters of a second and cuts through skin, spine, larynx, a vein, and an artery and then skin again (in that order); that it was invented because to execute everyone would have blunted all the swords in Paris (which I thought was quite poetic); that they did flatpack versions of the guillotine (Choppa, now available at Ikea); that otherwise genial looking elderly gents can start salivating into their beards when talking of axes slicing through muscle, bone, and sinew; and, most worryingly, that a joiner in London has built his own working guillotine. "It's easier to make a guillotine than gallows," he mused. Now, how do you suppose he knows that? I don't know about you, but I am frightened.

Gareth McLean in *The Guardian*, 19 December 2001

Lady Antonia Fraser had *One Pair of Eyes* (BBC2) and—if you'll forgive the male chauvinist piggery—very nice eyes they were. If you could concentrate on them while ignoring the programme, you had a chance of retaining consciousness throughout. If you couldn't, then the evening tended towards narcosis. The besotted director seemed suicidally intent on demonstrating Lady Antonia's versatility: shots of Lady Antonia walking were succeeded by shots of Lady Antonia talking, these in turn giving way to a virtuoso passage of Lady Antonia talking and walking simultaneously. Already stunned, the viewer was in no condition to remain unmoved when the screen suddenly erupted with the image of Lady Antonia typing.

Clive James in the *Observer*, July 1973

Gradually it dawned that this snickering, infantile voice belonged to the ubiquitous Julie Burchill, who claimed that she can't go down the corner shop without someone asking to marry her. No wonder the Antipodean crone was stunned into silence for a full ten seconds as she found herself being challenged, for once, by someone with a similar mindset. (I thought she'd walked out.)

Valerie Grove on a spat between Julie Burchill and Germaine Greer on *Woman's Hour*, in her *Wireless* column in *The Oldie*, April 1999 (issue 121)

It's bad enough that Comedy Central's monument to boorishness and arrested development makes pro wrestling look enlightened, or that it's wrecked *Win Ben Stein's Money* because now we know that Jimmy Kimmel, who works on both shows, really is as mean-spirited as he seems.

But the worst thing is, the fifth-graders who write this show are giving fifth-graders everywhere a bad name.

Rick Kushman of the Sacramento Bee, on *The Man Show*, December 1999— looking back at some of the worst TV of the year

Television? No good will come of this device. The word is half Greek and half Latin.

C. P. Scott

In the days of softer reality shows, back in 2000, a contestant on the original Survivor angrily called the two finalists a rat and a snake. Now the rats and the snakes are real, and the psychological machinations of Survivor seem positively civilized.

Caryn James in *The New York Times*, 4 February 2002

This episode felt like three or four subplots just jammed together by writers who were thinking, "maybe nobody will notice almost nothing is going on." Well, I think people noticed, so better luck next time.

Ultra Magnus on *Enterprise*, Episode 117 (Fusion)
on www.tnmc.org

The venue was Caesar's Palace in Las Vegas. It was jammed with celebrities, many of them still alive. The death rate during the course of the evening must have been fairly high, because it was obligatory to clap at every mention of Frank's outstanding qualities. During Stalin's speeches to the Praesidium the first delegate to stop clapping was routinely hauled off to be shot, but at Caesar's Palace peer-group pressure was enough to keep everyone clapping indefinitely…

Sadat and Begin both sent representatives. There could be no doubt Frank is a force for peace in the Middle East. Indeed, to hear Orson Welles tell it, Frank is practically the light of the world.

Clive James on *Frank Sinatra—the First Forty Years*
in the *Observer*, 17 February 1980

MTV is like a black hole… Nothing escapes it.
Marc Weingarten, author of *Station to Station*

The BBC had justified the sex scenes in Mr. Bragg's Bank Manager romance on the grounds that the production needed "fully to explore the characters as they experienced the possibilities of tenderness, love and fulfilment." It was not explained how artists in the past and many in the present, for that matter, had managed to explore such themes without resorting to explicit sex themes. But there we are.

Richard Ingrams on Melvyn Bragg's *A Time to Dance* in *The Oldie,* 3 April 1992 (no. 4)

Laying the triple-whammy on himself, Ian Holm as Oedipus signed off with "er, the gods curse all who disobey this charge" in the same way that a tired businessman remains yours sincerely. Alan Webb as Teiresias surged on in a wheelchair, simultaneously recalling *Dr. Strangelove* and the Mercury Theatre production of *King Lear*...

Clive James on the Cedric Messina production of *King Oedipus* (BBC2) in the *Observer,* 3 December 1972

In a season of truly awful mini-series—for instance, there was *Atomic Train*, which carried every hazardous material on Earth except banana peels—the saga of Noah stands out, and not just because his ark was attacked mid-flood by pirates.

This Noah fought a war, escaped a firebombed Sodom and Gomorrah, convinced God to save Lot, called down lightning to stop a human sacrifice, scared off a mob with lions and tigers and bears (oh, my), watched bad guys destroyed by a waterspout, and faced down the pirate captain who was, as everyone knows, good ol' Lot.

Both nights of the mini-series started with the warning that NBC took "poetic license with some events of the mighty epic of Noah and the flood." No kidding.

Rick Kushman of the *Sacramento Bee*, on NBC's *Noah's Ark*, December 1999—looking back at some of the worst TV of the year

"How do you hold a moonbeam in your hand?" sing the nuns with quizzical adoration, all unaware that the audience is singing a different question, to wit: is the Mother Superior being played by Charles Bronson?

> **Clive James** on a TV screening of *The Sound of Music* in the *Observer*, 31 December 1978

One thing I've learned from both *Star Trek* and *Moonbase* is that men are going to be wearing simple pullovers for ever. I never did think all that shoulder padding forecast by Hollywood in its science fiction would really catch on. I've also learned, not to my surprise, that women will continue to sport minis and plenty of décolletage whatever the stardate.

> **Bernard Hollowood** in *Punch*, 26 September 1973

Wuthering Heights (BBC2) is the blithering pits.

> **Clive James** in the *Observer*, 8 October 1978

It [*Dallas*] was plotted in conference, hammered out to prescription, screwed up to ever more lurid climaxes. JR was shot and, thanks to all the free publicity from the Wogans of the world, the programme attracted enormous ratings. A few years later, when the ratings were dipping, JR was shot again. Bobby was written out, run over and killed by a Cadillac, as befitted a son of the house of Ewing. Scarcely was he in his grave than it was decided they needed Bobby back. How to manage the resurrection? Everything that had happened since that fateful night, it was breezily explained, was a nasty dream.

> **Philip Purser** on *Dallas* in his book *Done Viewing* (Quartet Books, 1992).

This pretend news show is the worst of the prime time magazines that mistake crime, celebrities, and old-fashioned stupidity for news. It wouldn't be quite so bad if Stone "I'm the Tough Journalist" Phillips and Jane "No, I'm the Tough Journalist" Pauley didn't treat every story as if they were reporting from the lobby of the U.N. building.

Rick Kushman of the *Sacramento Bee*, on
Dateline NBC, December 1999 –
looking back at some of the worst TV of the year

The TV has gone into the "coming shortly, but just before that, and stay with us because after that we have… right then, let's talk about the next thing we're not going to do" routine, where everything stops before it's started. Coming up—not yet, of course—is the countdown to the execution of mass murdered Ted Bundy. The grotesque timetable reads like an afternoon's viewing on Grandstand.

Keith Floyd in *Floyd's American Pie* (BBC Books, 1989)

It is a matter of total indifference whether he [James Burke] is the way he looks—i.e., the right way up and practically exploding with pedagogic enthusiasm—or whether he is upside down, plugged into an electric socket, and all set to eat a live chicken…He is an image on your television screen that goes on and on supplying you with information you don't have. Merely turning the programme off is no good, since the after-image lingers on. You have to kick the set in even to slow him down.

Clive James in the *Observer*, 30 March 1980

Should P. J. Kavanagh in his *Journey Through Summer* (BBC1) have to pretend that he is a lone traveller? Or should he admit that he is at all times accompanied by cameramen, producer, and, possibly, dubbing mixers, continuity girls, researchers, lawyers, and accountants?

[…] He is seen in the distance, a remote creature silhouetted against the fading sky and miles from the nearest yokel or bumpkin. Occasionally his path is crossed by a team of hikers and a word or two are exchanged. And not one of the hikers puts a foot wrong or waves at the cameras or asks the producer when the programme will be on the telly because, naturally, they will all want to see it. And such behaviour strikes the viewer as extremely suspicious.

Bernard Hollowood in *Punch*, 25 July 1973

Elsinore was set in a velodrome…you kept expecting cyclists to streak past on the banking while the Prince was in mid-soliloquy.

Clive James on a BBC2 production of *Hamlet*, directed by Jonathan Miller, 1980, in the *Observer*, 1 June 1980

Why should people go out and pay money to see bad films when they can stay at home and see bad television for nothing?

Samuel Goldwyn, the *Observer*, 9 Sept 1956

Now that Hollywood writers and studios have negotiated their way out of a strike, the obvious question is: Does this mean TV will get better?

We've given this some serious thought, and we think we can truthfully say: Are you drunk?

Rick Kushman, May 2001

Dickens seems to be enjoying a new popularity among the made-for-television crowd, and viewers who stumble upon *Nickleby* tonight may be excused if they think they've tuned in Masterpiece Theater's *Oliver Twist* or *David Copperfield*. There's a look to these shows and these stories: everything's brown, nobody smiles, the characters seem unable to chew with their mouths closed.

Neil Genzlinger on *Nicholas Nickleby* in
The New York Times, 29 January 2002

Never in television history has there been anything so ... zzzzzzz. Sorry, fell asleep there, so boring. And CBS punished viewers with it six days a week. If there's any lesson, it's this: People brushing their teeth do not belong on television.

First the boring news: *Big Brother* is coming back for a second season.

Now the ray of hope: CBS remodeled the house.

And here's another thing: The chicken coop is gone. They booted the chickens. Nice touch. Those chickens were dragging down the show.

Rick Kushman on *Big Brother*

MTV today is an awesomely niched and segmented hydra, with half-hour blocks of programming for all the family—from non-stop Britney-pop for tweenies to greying VH1 mellowness for old farts who despised MTV in the first place.

James Slack for *Rock's Backpages*, July 2001—in an article entitled "Did Video Kill the Radio Star? MTV 20 years on"

Despite the unavoidable anachronism of a set of teeth whose fearful symmetry has been reflecting the sunlight like a heliograph since he first leapt to fame as the Crimson Pirate in 1952, Burt did a reasonable job of impersonating a patriarch.

His authoritative presence was reinforced by miracles. Dathan, a rat-faced heckler who had been stirring up trouble from the beginning of the series, was finally obliterated by a special effect. As a follow-up, Moses clobbered the Israelites with the aforesaid forty years' additional sentence. It was becoming increasingly hard to see why anybody should put up with him even for forty minutes, but before his credibility ran out there was just time to get him back up into the hills for a farewell chat with God.

The fact that God also spoke in Burt's voice permitted the charitable conjecture that Moses had been mentally disturbed all along. Some gory flashes-forward suggested that Operation Canaan would nevertheless proceed on schedule. Burt hit the dirt.

Clive James on Burt Lancaster in *Moses – the Lawgiver* (ATV) in the *Observer*, 27 February 1977

Here's the good news about a looming strike in Hollywood: The buzz—even strikes in Hollywood have buzz—is that writers and studios may reach a settlement before the clock strikes midnight May 1.

Here's the bad news: It's already too late to stop "Chains of Love."

"Chains of Love," a low-rent reality show, in case you're lucky and don't know, may be the stupidest thing on UPN, a network where competition for that title is fierce.

The show chains one "Picker"—their word, really—to four people of the opposite sex and they all flirt, date, and sleep together for a couple of days until a big guy who wears sunglasses even in the rain at night—again, really—forces the Picker to boot one date. Eventually there's only one person left chained to

the Picker, but if this week's premiere was any example, the real winner is the person let go first.
Rick Kushman of the *Sacramento Bee*, 26 April 2001

The Winter's Tale (BBC2) was worthily done, but one gets uncomfortable for the actors when they are surrounded by cubes and cones. You can't quell the fear that if one of them sits on a cone instead of a cube the blank verse will suffer.
Clive James in the *Observer*, 15 February 1981

Towering Inferno had met *The Poseidon Adventure*. Actors who had spent their whole lives on the feature list held on to their hair transplants and shouted the line that had been haunting them in their sleep for years: "We'll never make it!".
Clive James on a mini-series, *Condominium: When the Hurricane Struck,* in the *Observer*, 23 August 1981

Give an infinite number of monkeys an infinite number of typewriters and eventually they will come up with the complete works of Shakespeare. Give one chimp a laptop and, after a week or so, he will come up with the script for *Margaret: Royal Rebel* (Channel 5). At least, that's what you might think from the documentary's opening line: "The starting point of the life story of Princess Margaret is that she is a princess." Were it followed by the line "And her name is Margaret", you could have been forgiven for thinking you were watching some *People Like Us* spoof. As it was, the next line wasn't quite as idiotic (nor, indeed, as funny) as the first, so the cheap and cheerless film swung from dumb to dumber instead. [...]

125

A bland soup of recycled footage, rentagob talking heads and a conclusion that completely undermined the whole premise of the programme ("The idea that in any way she was a rebel is spurious," offered one biographer-type), *Margaret: Royal Rebel* was seasoned with that tabloid mixed spice of piety, deference and spite. All that documentary did illuminate was the fact that, in black-and-white times, most people had bad teeth.

Gareth McLean in *The Guardian*, 28 November 2001

The program's images of unruly teenage brains galloping out of control may instigate apprehension. Is Catcher about to morph into One Flew Over the Cuckoo's Nest? Will a lobotomy stop that teenage boy from belching at the breakfast table?

Don't worry. This deadpan Frontline report is aimed at soothing wounded parents reeling from the transformation of their sweet pups into sour curs. Just as they've been telling you, the poor dears can't help themselves. Their brain matter has turned into kudzu, overrunning the interior landscape of their teenage minds… A camera watches a sister and brother bicker while their mother sits beatifically nearby. At that moment you'd like to see "Inside the Maternal Brain," but she's as enigmatic as Mona Lisa.

Julie Salamon on *Inside the Teenage Brain* in
The New York Times, 31 January 2002

UC: Undercover (10 p.m. Sunday on NBC, Channel 3): Members of an elite Justice Department undercover squad get freaked out when they go undercover, wear head-to-toe black leather to blend in, and choke during the inevitable gunfights. Apparently, they don't understand the definition of "elite."

Rick Kushman of the *Sacramento Bee*, 28 September 2001

It is hard to tell where Pinter's characters come from: all you know is that they are on the way to Sidcup and are well informed about the bus routes leading through the Angel.

Clive James on a BBC2 production of *The Caretaker* in the *Observer*, 11 January 1981

One of my greatest pleasures in recent weeks has been operating a device called a Briketpresse which converts old newspapers into combustible products. [...]

I just keep wishing that there was some similar way in which television programmes could be recycled and put to good use. The nearest I can get to it is ripping up a copy of the Radio Times and soaking it; though you have to be careful here as the shiny advertising pages will not disintegrate in the water and have to be disposed of separately. Then there is all the publicity bumf that the BBC puts out which breaks up quite well, and which printed wastefully on one side only also makes quite good notepaper (in fact this article was originally drafted on it).

But there is really no beneficial side-effect that you can derive from your television set that would be like the newspaper bricks. The best thing you can do is to get rid of it altogether.

Richard Ingrams in the *Spectator*, 4 September 1982. Reprinted in *The Wit of the Spectator* (Century, 1989)

Rick Rockwell and Darva Conger, the happy couple from Fox's *Who Wants To Marry a Multi-Millionaire?*, the special that was part game show, part pirate auction, and all train wreck.

Sure, Rockwell, Conger, and 49 other women meticulously shed every scrap of dignity on the air, but the lovebirds weren't content to stop there. Rockwell—a.k.a. Restraining Order Rick—turned out to be only something of a multimillionaire and even less of a stand-up comic. Conger, who announced she wanted out of the spotlight, turned up on more talk shows than a presidential candidate and later posed nude for Playboy.

The real wonder is that these two didn't click.

Rick Kushman of the *Sacramento Bee*, December 2000 – looking back at some of the worst TV of the year

… all too apparently he has not grasped that beyond the trick of talking on television there is a further trick of talking and walking simultaneously, and that this trick must be mastered, not ignored.

Clive James on Carl Sagan presenting *Cosmos* in the *Observer*, 19 July 1981

In it [a radio quiz program called Hangperson], London's most moronic insomniacs phone and fail to answer questions no harder than "Name the first three letters of the alphabet, not necessarily in the correct order." It was simply unbearable. "A reindeer is a kind of deer, correct or incorrect?" "Can you spell nationalism?" "What is French for exit?" and so on. The hardest question of all was what exact date was the first episode of EastEnders, which nobody but a moron would know. All the contestants were soon stumped. But the most depressing aspect was that the question master never told them the correct answer. "Now, neoowww, that's not the answer Oim afride" he would whine.

Valerie Grove in her "Wireless" column in *The Oldie*, 20 March 1992 (no. 3)

Twin miracles of mascara, her eyes looked like the corpses of two small crows that had crashed into a chalk cliff.

Clive James on a TV interview with Barbara Cartland
in the *Observer*, 2 August 1981

Television is an invention that permits you to be entertained in your living room by people you wouldn't have in your home.

David Frost

Where do we start? The preposterous hype? The unrelenting incivility? The mean-spirited cracks intended as wit? Nah. Let's get to the analytical insight of color commentator, Minnesota Gov. Jesse "Surely Not The Brain" Ventura: "What a play!" "What a move!" "What a hit!" And, of course, "Oooohhh'" All in one game.

The XFL, really, was simply mediocre football in idiot packaging.

It set network television record lows for sports and prime-time ratings, and despite two-year contractual commitments from NBC and UPN, got canceled after one spectacularly uninspired season.

The highlight, however, occurred off the field when the hucksters turned on each other. XFL founder and chief con man Vince McMahon criticized Ventura for being—get this—too over the top.

Rick Kushman of the *Sacramento Bee*, on the XFL,
December 2001 – looking back at some of the
worst TV of the year

Working together as fatally as Laurel and Hardy trying to climb a wall, the script and the direction do a brilliantly thorough job of boiling Tolstoy's complexity of dialogue, commentary, and revealed action down to a simple narrative line which simultaneously faithfully reproduces and utterly betrays the novel's flow of events. "Papa's arranged a little dinner for my name day," breathes Hélène, her piercing boobs heaving in a frock closely resembling a two-car garage [...]. Pierre, valiantly played by Anthony Hopkins, can only goggle, bemused. Except when the occasional voice over supplies a brief stretch of interior monologue, goggling bemused is what Pierre goes in for full time. At Hélène's party, during which her sensational norks are practically on the table among the sweetmeats, Pierre is asked to do a worried version of the bug-eyed act Sid James turns on when he is abruptly shoved up against Barbara Windsor.

Clive James on the BBC's production of *War and Peace* in the *Observer*, 22 October 1972

The Weakest Link: Was there ever a show more defined by its name? ...

I'm not saying it might not be entertaining... but look at what we've got here.

A game show that tries to copy parts of *Who Wants To Be a Millionaire* and *Survivor* (the wrong parts, by the way) is hyping "stars" who've achieved nothing but insta-fame from appearing on a game show that *Link* is copying.

This is smoke, wisps with substance, and welcome to entertainment and celebrity in the 21st century. You don't know whether to weep for the fate of the world or throw up your hands and join the insanity.

Rick Kushman of the *Sacramento Bee*, 20 April 2001

On *Talk-In* (BBC1) Robin Day chaired a discussion of Miss World between a handful of Women's Libbers and the massed forces of darkness. Far from being the natural output of a male chauvinist pig, Day's arrogance goes beyond sex and indeed the bounds of credibility, to the point where you expected a flying wedge of ravening Maenads to spring from the audience and rip him to bits.

Clive James in the *Observer*, 10 December 1972

Music

Nothing is capable of being well set to music that is not nonsense.

Joseph Addison, British essayist, in *The Spectator*, which he cofounded (with Richard Steele) in 1711

He sang like a hinge.

Ethel Merman, on Cole Porter

Oddly combining designer chic sets with comic-strip costumes and characterisations for the Gauls. The stage is dominated by large stones (Gaulstones?), the drama is dissipated, and the singers are left to their own devices.

Charles Osborne on Bellini's opera Norma at the Royal Opera House, London, in the *Jewish Chronicle*, 27 February 1987

I do not mind what language an opera is sung in so long as it is a language I don't understand.

Sir Edward Victor Appleton
The Observer, "Sayings of the Week", 25 Aug 1955

Don't trouble yourself to play further. I much prefer the second.
Gioacchino Rossini to an aspiring composer
who wanted him to decide which of two
musical pieces he preferred

Too much counterpoint; what is worse, Protestant counterpoint.
Sir Thomas Beecham, of J. S. Bach,
The Guardian, 8 Mar 1971

Lorenz is good also in the Forging Songs, though the pace seems
rather sluggish. Perhaps the hammers are heavier at Bayreuth
than elsewhere.
Stephen Williams, in the *Evening Standard,*
December, 1936, on Max Lorenz in Richard Wagner's
opera Siegfried at the 1936 Bayreuth Festival

Nothing can be more disgusting than Oratorio. How absurd, to
see five hundred people fiddling like madmen about the Israelites
in the Red Sea!
Sidney Smith (1771–1845),
one time Canon of St Paul's Cathedral

It is, to put it bluntly, shockingly bad, and there were several moments during the evening when thoughts strayed affectionately back to Glyndebourne's notorious recent staging, dominated by its pile of manure.

That show at least had some ideas, but there is no evidence here of any constructive thinking about the characters or the action. Bjornson's set is a giant curved wall: for the opening scene it suggests an ossuary; for the end of the first act it revolves to reveal a garishly painted perspective view of a grand banqueting hall; it begins the second act as a mixture of bare bricks and concrete blocks. There's no statue, just something swinging about upstage that was not properly visible from where I was sitting. The fires of hell summoned by Robert Lloyd's Commendatore to claim Giovanni are a real display of pyrotechnics, complete with suspended flaming hand, but hardly of a piece with anything that precedes them.

Within that visual framework nothing meaningful happens at all. Bryn Terfel's Giovanni is just a bit of a lad, and his very deliberate murder of the Commendatore seems out of character for someone so totally lacking in guile. This Don is neither dangerous nor seductive, which is a bit of a problem in an opera that is all about danger and sex...

Colin Davis's monumentally slow conducting casts a pall over everything, and there are few signs that any of the characters have been properly defined. Rainer Trost's Ottavio is dry and unassertive. Adrianne Pieczonka's Anna is vocally capable, as is Melanie Diener's Elvira, though why she has to arrive in a sedan chair brandishing a telescope and a rifle escaped me.

The best singing comes from Rebecca Evans's sweetly toned Zerlina, and her scenes with Ashley Holland's over-thuggish Masetto do at least strike the right chords in an otherwise dreary evening. There's a total cast change next month, with Charles Mackerras taking over in the pit and Simon Keenlyside assuming the title role. Perhaps things might improve then.

Andrew Clements on Don Giovanni at the Royal Opera House, London, in the *Guardian,* 24 January 2002

At one point in the action, Giovanni urinates on the grave of the Commendatore—the production team has done something similar, metaphorically speaking, to Mozart's opera.

Charles Osborne on Don Giovanni at the London Coliseum, in the *Jewish Chronicle*, 21 April 1995

Foreigners liked us, though, and some claimed to be able to tell where one song stopped and the next one started, which was often more than we could.

Johnny Black member of the *Blacklight* band

The English may not like music—but they absolutely love the noise it makes.

Sir Thomas Beecham

Lovesexy, it has to be said, is a turgid collection of inconclusive riffs and weak melodies, decorated to distraction by harsh and flashy ornamentation.

David Toop on Prince (album *Love Sexy*) in the *Sunday Times,* 22nd May 1988

The third movement began with a dog howling at midnight, proceeded to imitate the regurgitations of the less-refined or lower-middle-class type of water-closet cistern, modulating thence into the mass snoring of a naval dormitory around dawn—and concluded inconsequentially with the cello reproducing the screech of an ungreased wheelbarrow.

Alan Dent on Bela Bartók

The sound of the harpsichord resembles that of a bird-cage played with toasting-forks.

Sir Thomas Beecham (attrib.)

Rossini would have been a great composer if his teacher had spanked him enough on his backside.

Ludwig Van Beethoven

Their lyrics are unrecognisable as the Queen's English.

Sir Edward Heath on the Beatles

Perhaps it was because Nero played the fiddle, they burned Rome.

Oliver Herford

This tragic bombardment of tuneless metal cliché fails to move in any direction other than towards the bin.

Steve Beebee on Debase (album *Domination*)
in *Kerrang*, October 2001

He knew music was Good, but it didn't sound right.

George Ade

Wagner's music is better than it sounds.

Mark Twain

Don gone wrong.

Charles Osborne's verdict on a production
of Mozart's opera, Don Giovanni

Madame Jenkins' recital [on 25 October 1944] was the incredible climax of a bizarre career. For Madame Jenkins' shortcomings as an artiste were nothing short of awesome. A dumpy coloratura soprano, her voice was not even mediocre—it was preposterous! She clucked and squawked, trumpeted and quavered. She couldn't carry a tune. Her sense of rhythm was uncertain. In the treacherous upper registers, her voice often vanished into thin air, leaving an audience with its ear cocked for notes with which she might just as well have never taxed her throat. One critic dolefully described her as "the first lady of the sliding scale." Peevishly remarked another: "She sounds like a cuckoo in its cups." ... Audiences laughed at her—laughed until the tears rolled down their cheeks, laughed until they stuffed handkerchiefs in their mouths to stifle the mirth —but she was never dismayed. Even when a song was punctured by rowdy applause (her listeners sometimes responded to a piercing clinker with whoops of "Bravo! Bravo!") the diva simply smiled and bowed. After all, she modestly murmured, didn't Frank Sinatra arouse the same sort of buoyant enthusiasm among his adoring bobby soxers?

Daniel Dixon on Florence Foster Jenkins in an article entitled "The Diva of Din"; in the December 1957 issue of *Coronet*

The music, even more so than Berkoff's play, is disposable stuff which sounds as though it was composed to be discarded after one hearing.

Charles Osborne on *Greek*, an opera by Mark-Anthony Turnage based on Stephen Berkoff's play of the same name

I like Wagner's music better than any other music. It is so loud that one can talk the whole time without people hearing what one says. That is a great advantage.

Oscar Wilde

It really is time for Barry White to find a couple of new angles on life and love. Despite the introduction of a variety of styles—pop, swingbeat, hip-hop beats, even reggae in a cover of Dean Martin's '50s hit *Volare*—a whole album of unrelieved deep-voiced avowals of lurve and devotion amid ever-present strings is positively exhausting. Part of the problem is that he's beginning to sound like a parody of himself, muttering trite nothings like "this is sensuous love" and "baby, I think I love your mind." By the time that other master of overkill Isaac Hayes puts in an appearance, things have reached ludicrous proportions as the pair growl love speeches— apparently to each other—and make medical history by "creating a fire that only your arms can quench." There's not even much of a decent song among all this sea of treacle.

Ian Cranna on Barry White's album *Put me in your mix* in *Q magazine,* December 1991

Mr. Ponthus's virtuosity is hair-raising, like beams of electricity shooting from a Frankenstein machine; but like those beams it has a kind of sameness. His emotional range was not as broad as his technical one; he alternated between a light touch and a full-throttle assault that left the listener breathless and somewhat battered.

Anne Midgette on pianist Marc Ponthus in *The New York Times,* 19 February 2002

The action takes place in what the director calls a "Time Tunnel," which I take to be a pretentious German way of describing the Washington DC subway, though Herr Friedrich has apparently also said that he got the idea for this "Ring" from the underground car park in Salzburg.

The tree in Hunding's apartment in the car-park or subway looks like a rocket poised for flight; Hunding himself comes home to his wife accompanied by six mafia-type henchmen...the Valkyries have ditched their horses to become a leather-clad female branch of Hell's Angels, who like to indulge in necrophiliac sex with the dead heroes they are supposed to be delivering to Valhalla.

Charles Osborne on Wagner's *Die Walküre* at the Royal Opera House, London, in the *Jewish Chronicle*, 6 October 1989

After four nights of the Ring, with the Ring of it still in our ears— which makes us look and feel quite savage—we deliberately say, "Never again with you, Wotan, Siegfried & Co!"

Punch on Wagner's *Ring Das Nibelungen*, May 1882

I only know two tunes. One of them is "Yankee Doodle" and the other isn't.

Ulysses S. Grant

Two encores including the thoroughly redundant *Eight Days A Week* and that certain first hit single (during which the curtain was dropped. Always gets the audience off, that). And that was it. Enough for Procol to have saved their skins with the second part of the show. Even so, the individual abilities, the subject matter of the number, and the general mystique, all promise so much more than is actually delivered. Bit like a Ploughman's Lunch, really.

Chris Salewicz on Procol Harum live at the London Palladium, in *New Musical Express,* 16 August 1975

Wagner has lovely moments but awful quarters of an hour.
Gioacchino Rossini, to Emile Naumann, April 1867

Wagner is evidently mad.

Hector Berlioz

Is Wagner a human being at all? Is he not rather a disease?
Friedrich Nietzsche

The Helen of Troy equivalent…is played by a drag artist…who, though he has modelled himself on *The Rocky Horror Show's* Frank N Furter, is not fit to lick Tim Curry's high heels.

The songs, weakly performed as send-ups of Abba, Gary Glitter, Donny Osmond et al (Al comes off best) are amplified beyond endurance. As the threat of hell loomed over poor Joe Soap, I found myself murmuring a line from Webster: "Why this is hell, nor am I out of it." Debit where debit is due: the show was devised by Maggie Norris and Paul Kerryson.

Charles Osborne on the musical *Hot Stuff* at the Lyric Hammersmith Studio, in the *Jewish Chronicle*, 27 August 1993

I like your opera. One day I think I'll set it to music.
Richard Wagner to an aspiring composer;
also attributed to Ludwig van Beethoven

Miss Truman is a unique American phenomenon with a pleasant voice of little size and fair quality…yet Miss Truman cannot sing very well. She is flat a good deal of the time…There are few moments during her recital when one can relax, and feel confident that she will make her goal, which is the end of her song.

Paul Hume, of the *Washington Post*, on a recital by Margaret Truman in 1950.

Does Ringo exist apart from his records? Who cares? It's doubtful the cutesy-pie tracks Richard Perry has turned into Ringo Records will ever move a listener to do anything more decisive than reach for the radio dial and that's what's so unnerving about these records. These cuts—this *No No Song*, that thoughtless remake of *Only You*, *Oh My My*, *You're Sixteen*—they're maddening only for their lack of personality, depth, emotional commitment. They're so insubstantial they're hardly fit objects to provoke boredom, much less concern and despair.

Gene Sculatti, *Creem,* March 1976

Jazz: Music invented for the torture of imbeciles.

Henry van Dyke

Like a foul alignment of all the black planets, this collection of 95–97 material culled from the *Keys To Ascension I and II* albums, saw all the important members of Yes […] reunited to wreak havoc on the world. Chords are played at random, tunes change tempo for no other reason than that is what happens in symphonies, and tracks are long just for longness's sake...The fact that they had a hit single as recently as 15 years ago should serve as a warning to us all that this sort of thing could strike at any moment.

David Quantick on the album *Keys to the Studio* by Yes in *Q magazine*, September 2001

Berlioz, musically speaking, is a lunatic; a classical composer only in Paris, the great city of quacks. His music is simply and undisguisedly nonsense.

Dramatic & Musical Review, 1843

This version takes place not in ancient Peking, but in the interior of a corrugated iron drum. Its characters are dressed in a variety of styles, ranging over 1,000 years of fashion. Some of them creep around in slow motion, while the young Prince of Persia, who is about to be executed, engages in simulated homoerotic sex with his executioner.

The courtiers Ping, Pang and Pong are portrayed as figures out of American vaudeville...and a huge banner in Act II informs us, unnecessarily and inaccurately, that "3 Enigmas = Death." It gets worse.

Charles Osborne on a production of Puccini's opera *Turandot* at the London Coliseum, 29 December 1995

Twenty-eight-year-old Lara Fabian is a huge star in France where cheesy chanteuses are cherished well into their dotage. Like Celine Dion, her speciality is MOR balladry delivered in a slightly adenoidal, vein-bulging, utterly characterless style. Producers Pat Leonard, Walter Afansieff, and Brian Rawlings—Madonna, Mariah Carey and Cher respectively—slap on their stock-in-trade shimmering chimes, cocktail synths, clanking key changes, and sanitised production, which marries Albinoni's baroque masterpiece with some lamentably bland lyrics.

Anna Britten on Lara Fabian's album
Lara Fabian in *Q magazine,* January 2001

Very vile—a catarrhal or sternutatory concerto. One frequently recurring phrase is a graphic instrumentation of a fortissimo sneeze, and a long passage is evidently meant to suggest a protracted, agonised bravura on the pocket handkerchief.

George Templeton Strong on a concerto by
Franz Liszt, diary entry

Classic music is th'kind that we keep thinkin'll turn into a tune.

Frank McKinney ("Kin") Hubbard,
Comments of Abe Martin and His Neighbors (1923)

The leader of cacophonists…is Arnold Schoenberg…He was ignored till he began to smash the parlor furniture, throw bombs, and hitch together ten pianolas, all playing different tunes, where-upon everybody began to talk about him. In Schoenberg's later works, all the laws of construction, observed by the masters, from Bach to Wagner, are ignored, insulted, trampled upon. The statue of Venus, the Goddess of Beauty, is knocked from its pedestal and replaced by the stone image of the Goddess of Ugliness, with the hideous features of a Hottentot hag.

Henry T. Finck, *Musical Progress*, 1923

Macho rap-rock from the UK. Horrible, horrible. This is the sound of five men in competition to prove who has the most testosterone.

Emma Johnston on "nu-metal" band Lillydamnwhite
(album *Eviscerate*) in *Kerrang*, July 2001

Liszt's orchestral music is an insult to art. It is gaudy musical harlotry, savage and incoherent bellowings.

Boston Gazette on Franz Liszt

There is not much acting to go with the voice; there hasn't been for a good few years now. The Covent Garden production, almost as venerable as the tenor himself, has been tailored to accommodate those famously frail knees. This Cavaradossi does not clamber up a scaffolding to paint his Madonna in the first act, but sits on a stool well downstage, painting a much smaller portrait on an easel. When he is shot at the end of the opera he subsides gently rather than dramatically to the ground, carefully cushioned all the way. This staging began life in 1964 and the sets look as if only paint is holding them together, while the ages of this trio of principals suggest that the sponsorship department at the ROH missed a trick by not getting Saga Holidays to underwrite it this time.

Andrew Clements on Luciano Pavarotti's performance
in *Tosca* at the Royal Opera House, London,
in the *Guardian,* 14 January 2002

I can compare *Le Carnaval Romain* by Berlioz to nothing but the caperings and gibberings of a big baboon, over-excited by a dose of alcoholic stimulus.

George Templeton Strong, diary entry

Composition indeed! Decomposition is the proper word for such hateful fungi!

Dramatic and Musical World on Franz Liszt, 1855

Unfortunately the production, which is the silliest I have encountered of any opera, does a serious disservice to the composer...Instead of staging the story which Rossini set to music, the producer (Keith Warner) has placed the opera in a twentieth-century Middle East, with the characters transformed into modern political leaders, and Moses, for some reason, dressed to resemble Mr. Billy Connolly. When a group of extras appeared from the stalls in Act I, training machine-guns upon the principals and chorus, I almost wished they had instead had the production team in their sights.

Charles Osborne on Rossini's opera *Moses*,
in the *Jewish Chronicle*, 31 January 1986

Oh dear, oh dear. Second-rate teeny acts (Samantha Mumba, a1, S Club 7) or people who promised never to trouble us again (Lulu, Lisa Stansfield, Yazz, Erasure) sing Motown songs badly. And what on earth the admirable Chris Rea—neither second-rate nor teen fodder—is doing here is something he should be discussing with his advisors right now; as he sacks them.

John Aizlewood on *Motown Mania*,
by various artists, in *Q magazine*, March 2001

A squeak's heard in the orchestra
The leader draws across
The intestines of the agile cat
The tail of the noble hoss.

G. T. Lanigan: *The Amateur Orlando* (1875)

I allowed twenty-four hours to elapse before writing this review: if I had been forced to produce it immediately after leaving the opera house, my language would have been distressingly intemperate. To put it mildly, then, this was the worst production that I can remember having experienced of any opera, and the only completely unmoving one of *Fidelio*…

Throughout the evening, the stage looked an absolute mess, comically so when the grim reaper and the devil arrived in stilts in the final scene. The audience, which until then had behaved itself surprisingly well, finally hooted with glee when the devil's curtains managed to close around Pizarro only with a little help from Pizarro himself.

I do advise the hard-hearted to go and see this *Fidelio*: they'll have a good laugh.

Charles Osborne on Beethoven's opera *Fidelio* at the Royal
Opera House, London, in the *Jewish Chronicle*,
11 July 1986—in an article entitled
"Is there a doctor in the House?"

In the 18-year wake of David Bowie's *Pin-Ups*, few artists have been foolish enough to "do" a covers album. Duran Duran were the last notable culprits with 1995's inexplicable *Thank You*; and now Simple Minds have decided to come after them… Really, to call this a turkey would be unfair to the birds who share the same name.

John Harris on the album *Neon Lights* by
Simple Minds in *Q magazine*, October 2001

I assure you that the typewriting machine, when played with expression, is not more annoying than the piano when played by a sister or near relation.

Oscar Wilde, letter to Robert Ross
from Reading Gaol, 1 April 1897

I nearly trod in some once.

Sir Thomas Beecham, on Stockhausen

I liked the bit about quarter to eleven.

Erik Satie on "From Dawn to Noon on the Sea"
from *La Mer* by Claude Debussy

A primitive example of opera when it was a minimalist musical form, before it had fully climbed out of the slime of heightened recitative in which it had its beginnings.

Charles Osborne on Monteverdi's opera
The Return of Ulysses

Specifically, this is the sound of bear-like backwoods beard-wearers desperately trying to shout empty bourbon bottles full, while stumbling haphazardly about a guitar-filled garage in the belligerent and boisterous manner of an insensible quartet of hillbilly Father Jacks.

Ian Fortnum on Antiseen (album *Boys from Brazil*)
in *Kerrang*, October 2001

What a giftless bastard! It annoys me that this self-inflated mediocrity is hailed as a genius. Why, in comparison with him, Raff is a giant, not to speak of Rubinstein, who is after all a live and important human being, while Brahms is chaotic and absolutely empty dried-up stuff.

Peter Tchaikovsky on German composer
Johannes Brahms, in his diary, 1886

I love Wagner; but the music I prefer is that of a cat hung up by its tail outside a window and trying to stick to the panes of glass with its claws.

Charles Baudelaire

Instead of being told never to darken Bow Street again, Herr Schaaf was invited back to do his worst. I sincerely hope that this is, indeed, his worst, and that we are not going to have forced upon us a long line of increasingly ridiculous productions of Mozart's operas, the line stretching in an unbroken sequence to the crack of doom.

Idomeneo… is here reduced to a shambles. Let one example— and that by no means the most absurd—suffice: while singing a gentle andante in which she happily anticipates her journey to her homeland, Elizabeth Connell is obliged to indulge in some ludicrous business with a small boy in overalls who is carrying a can of paint and a paintbrush. After much ogling and embarrassing by-play, she— still singing—manages to get the paint-pot away from him, and proceeds to daub the floor of the stage with lashings of red paint.

From my seat in the stalls I was unable to see what she was scrawling; but had I been Ms Connell it would have been some obscene and impractical advice to the director.

Charles Osborne on a production of Mozart's opera
Idomeneo at the Royal Opera House, London, reviewed in the
Jewish Chronicle, 8 December 1989

Yeah, some of them are about ten minutes long, others five or six.
Bob Dylan, when asked in an interview
to say something about his songs

Three tracks into this truly lamentable opus and you'll have lost
the will to live; four tracks and you'll be weeping openly into your
coffee cup.
James Cooper on heavy metal band Solstice
(album *Lamentations*) in *Kerrang*, August 2001

The audience seemed rather disappointed; they expected the
ocean, something big, something colossal, but they were served
instead with some agitated water in a saucer.
Louis Schneider on *La Mer* by Claude Debussy

Wagner, thank the fates, is no hypocrite. He says right out what
he means, and he usually means something nasty.
James G. Huneker

Critics have had fun trying to explain the symbolism of
Brunnhilde with a brown-paper bag over her head, and the
charred figure emerging from the non-flames at the end. My
guesses are that the brown-paper bag was for a take-away
Brunnhilde, and that the dark figure was Baron Samedi, a person-

age who, in voodoo mythology, presages death, highly appropriate for this staging.

Charles Osborne on Wagner's *Götterdämmerung*
at the Royal Opera House, London, 3 November 1995

This production by Andrei Konchalovsky in his company debut is dominated by a rotating domelike platform upon which all the action is staged. In effect the entire cast, which also includes 120 choristers, 41 dancers, and 227 supernumeraries as well as a horse, a dog, and a goat, perform the work atop a hill. It was hard to watch the stage without worrying that someone was going to fall into the orchestra pit. Sure enough, with about six minutes left in the final scene, that's what happened.

Anthony Tommasini on an operatic production of
War and Peace in *The New York Times*, 16 February 2002

This month's award for The Album Most Destined to Become an Ashtray is *Top TV Themes* by the Tony Osborne Sound…Mr. Osborne had "chart success" last year with his arrangement of one of Canteloube's *Songs of the Auvergne* better known as the Dubonnet Ad music to the man in the street, or rather, the man at home watching the telly.

Barry Fantoni in *Punch*, October 1976

Shall I be able to sit out the whole of these 351 pages quietly, without wanting my money back?

When I have seen it all, and want to air the fact the next time I dine out, shall I be utterly stumped by those beastly German names?

What on earth are Nibelungs? Have they anything to do with the man who plays the bassoon?

How will they manage this? "Fasolt and Fafner enter", I quote from the book, "both of giant's stature." Then they sing a duet. Will this do in alto, on stilts, and in pantomime heads, or how?

Punch on Wagner's *Ring Das Nibelungen*, May 1882

What the Marx Brothers did to Verdi's *Il trovatore* in *A Night at the Opera*, ENO has now done to the same composer's *A Masked Ball* at the London Coliseum…This production is set neither in the Sweden of Verdi's original intention nor the Boston for which he settled because of censorship restrictions—but in what looks like a derelict lunatic asylum whose former inmates are still loitering about.

Charles Osborne on Verdi's opera *Un Ballo in Maschera* at the London Coliseum, in the *Jewish Chronicle*, 29 September 1989

Some time ago, in this space, I attempted to cheer up others, who felt Life closing in on them with nothing accomplished, by writing that Napoleon never saw a steamboat until he was fifty-eight and that Mozart never wrote a bar of music until he was ninety.

A very pleasant lady correspondent has written in to ask me if there has not been some mistake. She has always understood, she says, that Mozart died at the age of thirty-five and that he began to compose at the age of four.

I don't believe that we can be thinking of the same Mozart. The Mozart that I meant was Arthur Mozart, who lived at 138th street until he died, in 1926, at the age of ninety-three.

Robert Benchley, "Back to Mozart," in
The Benchley Roundup, a selection by
Nathaniel Benchley (Cassell, 1956)

It is a slow-moving opera, the extreme length of which is dispro-portionate to its musical and dramatic worth.

Charles Osborne on Wagner's opera
Theodora, 20 February 1999

Instrumental music from performers who have overestimated themselves is a peculiarly annoying experience. So, if Unwed Sailor eat, it will be because audiences throw food at them. Their particular brand of aural frustration is dominated by Johnathon Ford's densely chording bass elaborately jabbering nothing in par-ticular in technically complicated interweave with Nicholas Tsei's guitar. A drummer thrashes along aimlessly. Synthesizer drones and howls plug the gaps—for some reason swinging horribly from earphone to earphone on a piece called Riddle of Stars. When, eventually, one of them does sing…it's so pallid you want to give him a good shaking.

Phil Sutcliffe on Unwed Sailor's album
The Faithful Anchor in *Q magazine*, September 2001

Now, I haven't thought very highly of Beethoven in the past. His work has seemed a bit thick and straining to me, not unlike a dull but efficient exhibition of weight-lifting; nor do I care for his endings, with enough repetitions of the common chord to make me yell "All right, all right." But this new light on the man sends my respect shooting up. A composer who can juggle the reed, brass, and catgut to convey his belief in human rights is fully entitled to have his scaled-down bust on the top of school pianos.

Basil Boothroyd on Beethoven's *Egmont Overture* in "Can you read music" from *The Whole Thing's Laughable* (George Allen & Unwin, 1964)

Artistically, Schubert comes before us in it as almost the typical example of the self-taught genius, with the reservation, however, that he did not teach himself enough.

The Edinburgh Review, no. 324, October 1883

David Alden, the director who has been responsible for some of the English National Opera's most ridiculously awful productions, was reported as saying: "If the stage direction says 'she weeps,' I like her to be laughing. That's the way my mind works. It's a favourite creative trick of mine."

Trick, yes, but creative it certainly isn't.

Charles Osborne, March 1996 – in an article entitled "Disaster Aria"

There is very little more to be said. The introduction is not without interest: the fugues very nearly are. The Mendelssohn fugues are—rather ordinary Mendelssohn; and the Wesley—well, we should all be glad to write almost any sort of a fugue in our 72nd year.

The Consort on publication of *Three Organ Fugues*
by Samuel Wesley and Dr. Mendelssohn. No. 22, July 1965

The "Mode" made very dubious puffing noises as though they were blowing up a paddling pool.

Smash Hits on Depeche Mode

The clumsiness of the title of Glass's opera (for which presumably one must blame his librettist, Doris Lessing) is indicative of the styleless banality of the entire enterprise. Planet 8, a typical product of the drug era, is a kind of Acid House for grown-ups…Doris Lessing's allegorical libretto, whose subject is the physical death of a planet and its spiritual renewal, is of an awesome dullness, couched in tedious and platitudinally flat language.

Charles Osborne on Philip Glass's opera *The Making of the Representative for Planet 8* at the London Coliseum, in the *Jewish Chronicle*, 26 November 1988—in an article entitled "Bye, bye art – hullo trendiness"

Too many notes.

Joseph II on Mozart's music (attrib.)

They boast a fey vocalist singing wretch-worthy lyrics about love and freedom and beautiful people to the accompaniment of the ubiquitous funky drum beat and swathes of swirling guitar. After a while this all becomes too predictable, too tacky, too much... Even with INXS producer Pete Lorimer adding a certain professional gleam to the proceedings, this is still an album that becomes more unlistenable the more it is listened to.

David Roberts on the album *People* by
The Apples in *Q magazine,* October 1991

I did not watch the Brit awards on television last night. Recent experience suggests that such back-slap-athons are hazardous to my blood pressure. Indeed, simply reading about the Brits was quite enough to send me into a state of foaming apoplexy. Kylie, Dido, Travis, Westlife, S Club 7, Shaggy... and, topping it all off, Sting, emperor of wine-bar muzak. It was a line-up to make you howl, or at least despair of pop ever meaning anything, well, meaningful again...

Chart pop has become so redundant, so musically bankrupt, that the best we can do is collude with the mass delusion that a pocket-sized Oz automaton is a spunky sex goddess with a flawless sense of irony. I refer, of course, to Ms Minogue, whose numbingly formulaic 'Can't Get You Out of My Head' is being hailed as some work of postmodern electro-pop genius... In the new global celebrity culture, pop literally means nothing other than fame.

Barney Hoskyns, Editorial Director of *Rock's Backpages*
(www.rocksbackpages.com) in the *Independent,* 22 Feb 2002

157

I am delighted to add another unplayable work to the repertoire. I want the Concerto to be difficult and I want the little finger to become longer. I can wait.

Arnold Schoenberg

Everyone gestures in sign language as well as singing, as though they are performing to an audience of the deaf-and-dumb.

Charles Osborne on a production of Handel's oratorio *Theodora*, 24 May 1996—in an article "Hard to Handel"

The still-born brainchild of Korn bassist Reginald "Fieldy" Arvizu, *Rock 'n' Roll Gangster* is an utterly unlikeable gangsta-rap pastiche. When not tiresomely trumpeting his titanic weed intake, Fieldy stumbles through sterilised sex rhymes and banal B-boy bragging so devoid of charm or wit that they make the similarly salacious Kid Rock sound like Stephen Fry in comparison. Meanwhile minor-league guest rappers and the tinny, tired production pole-axe any pretensions the project has towards hip-hop credibility. Despite 2002 still being very much in its infancy, the chances of a record worse than this one being released by a major label all year are exceedingly slim.

Dan Silver on the album *Rock 'n' Roll Gangster* by Fieldy's Dreams in *Q magazine*, January 2002

The musical equivalent of St Pancras station.

Sir Thomas Beecham on Edward Elgar's *Symphony in A Flat*

Difficult do you call it, Sir? I wish it were impossible.

Samuel Johnson on the performance of a celebrated violinist; William Seward Supplement to the Anecdotes of Distinguished Persons (1797)

Splitting the convulsively inflated larynx of the Muse, Berg utters tortured mistuned cackling, a pandemonium of chopped-up orchestral sounds, mishandled men's throats, bestial outcries, bellowing, rattling, and all other evil noises…Berg is the poisoner of the well of German music.

Berlin Germania on Alban Berg

If I had to make up my mind immediately as to whether Mr. Birtwistle was a genius or merely a plodder with chutzpah, I would be too embarrassed to answer.

Charles Osborne on Harrison Birtwistle's opera *The Mask of Orpheus*, in the *Jewish Chronicle*, 30 May 1986

Like Parsifal but without the jokes.

Sir Thomas Beecham on Hans Pfitzner's opera *Palestrina* (attrib.)

The kind of opera that starts at six o'clock and after it has been going three hours you look at your watch and it says 6.20.

David Randolph on Wagner's opera *Parsifal*

Being 13 was never as vapid as this. If it had been, we would all be traffic wardens by now.

Melody Maker on the pop group Bros

Like two skeletons copulating on a corrugated tin roof.

Sir Thomas Beecham on the harpsichord

… sad old traditionalists who enjoy some semblance of a tune will find little comfort here. Actually, no, that's not fair: there are hundreds of tunes here, it's just that they're all being played at once and the overall effect is like a jazz band playing thrash tunes as they fall down a flight of stairs. Bloody horrible.

Mörat on Spazztic Blurr (album *Spazztic Blurr*) in *Kerrang*, October 2001

It is a music one must hear several times. I am not going again.

Gioacchino Rossini of *Tannhäuser*

The booing, which began at the interval and virtually drowned the applause at the final curtain, was aimed solely at the director…The silly man looked pleased at the reception he got, like a naughty child delighted at having shocked Mum and Dad.

Charles Osborne on Meyerbeer's *Les Huguenots* at the Royal Opera House, London, in the *Jewish Chronicle*, 15 November 1991

From the first oafish gothic crash of *Black Sabbath* it was clear this band was dumb. Really intensely dumb. Even in that first hearing there was something in Ozzy's hammy Jack Bruce-and-beyond larynx, in the stonefaced simplicity of Tony Iommi's lost chords, in Geezer's globular lines, and Bill Ward's sub-Bonham stomp. Something that spelled sublime idiocy. This wasn't the Black Sabbath of Mario Bava and Boris Karloff, it was drive-in Herschell Gordon Lewis.

Barney Hoskyns and Gregg Turner on Black Sabbath, *Creem*, 1982

Some cry up Haydn, some Mozart,
Just as the whim bites; for my part
I care not a farthing candle
For either of them, or for Handel.

Charles Lamb, "Free Thoughts on Several Eminent Composers" (1830)

What can you do with it? It's like a lot of yaks jumping about.
Sir Thomas Beecham on the third movement
of Beethoven's *Seventh Symphony*

A carpenter's hammer, in a warm summer noon, will fret me into
more than midsummer madness. But those unconnected, unset
sounds are nothing compared to the measured malice of music.
Charles Lamb, *Elia* (1823)

The director, Tim Albery, has succeeded in totally obscuring the
opera's clear narrative line, to no discernible purpose.
Charles Osborne on a production of
Verdi's opera *Nabucco*, 26 April 1996

The only sensual pleasure without vice.
Samuel Johnson, referring to music

I mean, it can't be that difficult to come up with 800 words on
any gig. A beginning, a middle, and an end, with a couple of
twiddly bits in between isn't too much to ask. Normally. But then
this was Television. Nothing rhymed. Nothing reasoned. Two days

on and my brain is offal. Every idea heads for the slop bucket. Still, I think, I think that...

Television, the heavily publicised seminal band (?) of the late Seventies, attracted probably the smallest turn-out at the City Hall since they last toured here.

They were wrecked with jet-lag and groping their way towards acquaintance with a sound man and a system they had met 24 hours earlier.

They played one of the most erratic sets I have ever heard and further eroded the sympathies of the small crowd by interminable tuning up, provoking cries of "Get on with it!" even from the most devoted. ...Perhaps ten minutes after they started the first of a steady stream of people walked out on them, though I think most of these were local liggers lacking the incentive of having laid their money down.

Around me for the first four numbers brows were knit, noses crinkled, and lips curled as their owners complained about the dire quality of the sound, which was all snarly and rough as if it was being spewed out of a cement mixer.

> **Phil Sutcliffe** on the band Television live at City Hall,
> Newcastle, Sounds, 1978

Others, even if they know the play, will be lucky to catch from the entire opera more than a few words of the composer's inconsequential vocal line above the overwrought cacophony that passes for musical instrumentation.

> **Charles Osborne** on *Timon of Athens* in the
> *Jewish Chronicle*, 24 May 1991—in an article entitled
> "Timon is just a waste of time"

Attempting to thank the band and the Fillmore staff, he's inter-
rupted by audience calls for more. [He responds with] "For one
time, if you want to applaud, fine, but instead of yelling 'more and
more and more,' why don't you try sometime... the musicians
are here; leave it up to them, and don't be assholes all the time...
just leave it hang, and leave it up to them, OK? [heavy sarcasm:]
MORE MORE MORE MORE MORE... just hang out, OK?" I
reckon the audience know exactly what they were doing, and
regard getting a rise out of Bill Graham as part of the entertainment. This is New York after all.

Mark Pringle on The Grateful Dead for
Rock's Backpages, April 2001

Watching The Villains' Opera last week at the Olivier, a number
of questions popped into my head. Who sanctioned it? What did
it cost? And would such a soft-brained piece of twaddle ever have
passed through the sieving process if it hadn't come in the guise
of a would-be popular musical, the Holy Grail that these days we
are all meant to worship?

[...] By March 2001 the NT will have brought us no fewer
than five musicals in less than two years: *Candide* (excellent),
Honk! The Ugly Duckling (mediocre), *The Villains' Opera* (dire),
with *Singin' in the Rain* to come this summer and *My Fair Lady,*
in association with Cameron Mackintosh, next spring. Am I
alone in finding this devotion to tune-and-toe shows
somewhat excessive?

Michael Billington in the *Guardian,* 19 April 2000,
in an article on the National Theatre, London,
entitled "The villain's repertory"

It has no more real pretension to be called music than the jangling and clashing of gongs and other uneuphonious instruments with which the Chinamen, on the brow of a hill, fondly thought to scare away our English blue-jackets.

The Musical World on Richard Wagner's *Lohengrin*

Failure seemed to go to their heads...Another failure, Boettcher's production on the Beach Boys' only venture into disco—1979's *Here Comes The Night*—prompted the pair to create an entire disco-meets-Beach Boys album. Boettcher's saccharine melodies and fey vocals are rendered even camper by disco rhythms and the fruity whole is as over-ripe as its title suggests. While Boettcher's version of the "Banana Boat Song" has to heard to be believed, its lack of release until now could be regarded as a mercy killing.

Toby Manning on Gary Usher's album
Add Some Music To Your Day in *Q magazine*, August 2001

The music of Wagner imposes mental tortures that only algebra has a right to inflict.

Paul de Saint-Victor on Richard Wagner in *La Presse*

The Beatles are not merely awful, I would consider it sacrilegious to say anything less than that they are godawful.

William F. Buckley Jr.

Buller, whom I can hardly call promising since he is already in his mid-60s, has composed vocal lines of an excruciating dullness accompanied by nondescript orchestral noise devoid of imagination.

Charles Osborne on John Buller's first opera *The Bacchae* at the London Coliseum, in the *Jewish Chronicle*, 15 May 1992

I would like to take up this afternoon an analysis of Bach's (Carry Me Back to Old Virginny) symphonic tschaikovski in C minor, one of the loveliest, and, at the same time, one of the most difficult exercises for three-and-a-half fingers ever written. I may have to stop and lie down every few minutes during my interpretation, it is so exciting. You may do as you like while I am lying down.

In the first place, I must tell you that the modern works of Schönberg, although considerably incomprehensible to the normal ear (that is, an ear which adheres rather closely to the head and looks like an ear) are, in reality, quite significant to those who are on the inside. This includes Schönberg himself, his father, and a young man in whom he confides while dazed. What you think are random noises made by the musicians falling over forward on their instruments are, when you understand them, really steps in a great, moving story—the Story of the Travelling Salesman who came to the Farmhouse. If you have heard it, try to stop me.

Robert Benchley, "How to Understand Music," in *The Benchley Roundup*, a selection by Nathaniel Benchley (Cassell, 1956)

The director…opted for one of those heavily symbolic productions designed to prevent the audience from ever finding out what is supposed to be happening.

Charles Osborne on a production of Verdi's opera *Jérusalem*, in the *Jewish Chronicle*, 4 May 1990

Food & Drink

"Take them away. You wouldn't expect this in a transport caff," I said to John Rogers, the assistant dining-room manager. He left and came back with new glasses. No apology. Just a sneer. "I think it came from the orange juice, sir," he said, referring to the dirt.

I've been dining in great hotels (which *Cliveden* certainly isn't) for well over 50 years. I can tell lipstick and smear-dirt from orange juice...

Knowing they were in for trouble, the hotel banned me. That's like being told I'm not welcome at the ladies' toilet in Middlesborough railway station. I wasn't going there either.

Michael Winner. From *Winner's Dinners*
(Robson Books, 2000)

They make a rare Soop they call Pepper-Pot; it's an excellent Breakfast for a Salamander, or a good preparative for a Mountebank's Agent, who Eats Fire one day, that he may get better Victuals the next. Three Spoonfuls so Inflam'd my Mouth, that had I devour'd a Peck of Horse-Radish, and Drank after it a Gallon of Brandy and Gunpowder, I could not have been more importunate for a Drop of Water to cool my Tongue.

Edward Ward

The dietary arrangements on the original ark are not vouch-safed by Genesis. My hunch is that the 300-cubit-long vessel pretty soon turned into a floating abattoir, a water-borne version of the Paris Zoo during the siege of that city. But I may be wrong. I await your letters. I do hope, though, for their sake, that Noah and his centenarian sons ate better than visitors to the shack Ark.

Jonathan Meades on *The Ark*, London W8, in
The Times, 11 April 1994

For most, it's a last resort offering heartburn-on-a-plate chow and slower-than-a-snail service at expensive-for-what-it-is tabs; in sum, "spare yourself."

Review of the *T.G.I. Friday's* chain in *Zagat* 2002

Cauliflower is nothing but cabbage with a college education.

Mark Twain

It seems an unusual desire, to create a restaurant that looks like a book-jacket, and most of the cooks from whom Mrs. David originally acquired her recipes would think it even more unusual to learn to cook from a book instead of from Mum. But all this must spring naturally from the kind of second-order experience that lies behind the cult of food. Alice Waters is a girl from New Jersey who earned her culinary stripes by resolutely cooking her way through a compendium of French recipes assembled by an Englishwoman, using ingredients from Northern California and serving them up to the me-generation in a restaurant named after an old movie. The result is a Franco-Californian cuisine of almost ludicrous refinement, in which the simplest item is turned into an object of mystification. A ripe melon, for example, is sought for as if it were a piece of the True Cross. Ms. Waters applauds herself on serving one: "Anyone could have chosen a perfect melon, but unfortunately most people don't take the time or make an effort to choose carefully and understand what that potentially sublime fruit should be." She talks as if selecting a melon were an existential choice of a kind to leave Jean-Paul Sartre stumped.

Angela Carter on the *Chez Panisse Menu Cookbook* by Alice Waters, in the *London Review of Books*, 1984

A cucumber should be well sliced, and dressed with pepper and vinegar, and then thrown out, as good for nothing.

Samuel Johnson

Mass-produced food, poor service, and a cold atmosphere— brickbats abound for the cavernous relaunched Liverpool Street hotel dining room which has London's "leading" restaurant name behind it—"Conran c**p at Conran prices," as one reporter more succinctly put it.

Report on *Aurora,* Harden's London Restaurants 2001

The bar remains a Daytonian-spring-break beer blast with Windsor knots. A hand-over-fist gold mine. But when it comes to dining, *Guastavino's* wants respect. And recognition. And a place around the table of restaurants that matter. And considering the enormity of the enterprise (two dining rooms plus private spaces can accommodate 600), the house has moved at breakneck pace to produce proper credentials. Already, it boasts a staff that must have been drilled harder than Demi Moore in GI Jane to achieve this level of attention over this large a playing field. ...A lot of gastronomic ground is covered, perhaps with a few too many sprints.

Those matzo balls are good, the broth thick with vegetables, but is there a Jewish bubbe that ever used this little fat?

Hal Rubenstein on Terence Conran's *Guastavino's* in
New York Magazine, 3 April 2000

Why do they always put mud into coffee on board steamers? Why does the tea generally taste of boiled boots?

William Makepeace Thackeray

It is fair to say that Marco Pierre White is unencumbered by false or any other kind of modesty. His new restaurant is called *Marco Pierre White: The Restaurant*—in order, no doubt, to distinguish it from Marco Pierre White: The Cuddly Toy and Marco Pierre White: The Snow-boots with Funny Laces.

Jonathan Meades in the *Times Saturday Review*,
8 January 1994

Free yourselves from the slavery of tea and coffee and other slopkettle.

William Cobbett

I was distracted by my friend's filet mignon sandwich. Could I trust a steakhouse that serves a flavorless cut like filet mignon as its special? Dessert answered that. A single scoop of tangerine sorbet arrived in a giant round bowl. I peered in, and it reminded me of a pebble at the bottom of a well.

It made me think of what Tim Zagat, a founder of Restaurant Week, said. "It's in the interest of the restaurant to do it well," he said. "If the restaurant goes cheap, the restaurant is just damaging its own image."

Indeed. Next time, I'll buy a hot dog and take in the view from the terminal steps.

Amanda Hesser on *Michael Jordan's: The Steak House* in Grand Central Terminal, in *The New York Times*, 6 February 2002—in an article entitled *"The $20.02 Lunch: A Taste of the Town, or Letdown City?"*

⁂

The catering trade is laughingly called the hospitality industry. That's a joke. Any less hospitable industry would be hard to find. The frequent receptionist greeting "Have you got a reservation?" typifies the arrogance of many restaurants... How many times are you greeted in a restaurant with a smile? A smile to most restaurant employees is like a silver cross to a vampire.

Michael Winner in his introduction to *Winner's Dinners* (Robson Books, 2000)

⁂

The potatoes looked as if they had committed suicide in their own steam. There were mashed turnips, with a glazed surface, like the bright bottom of a tin pan. One block of bread was by the lonely plate. Neither hot nor cold, the whole aspect of the dinner table resisted and repelled the gaze, and made no pretensions to allure it.

George Meredith

⁂

None of Liebrandt's peculiar touches, however, prepared me for the outlandish goofiness of the desserts. The creations are mostly ethereal flans, foams, and gelées made with ingredients like Pepsi, mentholyptus, or Guinness stout. The Guinness is served in jellied form, as part of a tasteless flan made with orange water; the Pepsi is reduced down, then dripped over a kind of frothy, whiskey-flavored zabaglione. I'm not sure either of them tasted very good, but then, that's not always the point at *Papillon*. Spectacle is the point, and in the end, you can't help enjoying the show.

Adam Platt on *Papillon* in *New York Magazine*,
4 February 2002

When I ask for a watercress sandwich, I do not mean a loaf with a field in the middle of it.

Oscar Wilde to a waiter, recorded by Max Beerbohm
in a letter to Reggie Turner, 15 April 1893

Some still think the "too trendy" scene justifies a trip to this large Art Deco basement, off Piccadilly Circus; it's living off the bar's former reputation, though, and—thanks to "evil" cooking and "rude" service—many reporters just find a visit here "deeply depressing."

Report on *Atlantic Bar & Grill*,
Harden's London Restaurants 2002

Anchovies: I met my first anchovy on a pizza in 1962, and it was seven years before I mustered the courage to go near another. I am known to cross a street whenever I see an anchovy coming. Why would anybody consciously choose to eat a tiny, oil-soaked, leathery maroon strip of rank and briny flesh?

Jeffrey Steingarten on "My food phobias" in his introduction
to *The Man Who Ate Everything* (Alfred A. Knopf, Inc., 1997)

They gave us for dinner boiled ant-bear and red monkey; two dishes unknown even at Beauvilliers in Paris, or at a London city feast. The monkey was very good indeed, but the ant-bear had been kept beyond its time; it stank as our venison does in England; and so, after tasting it, I preferred dining entirely on monkey...

Charles Waterton

Still hungry for the bivalve that lifted Aphrodite from the sea and encouraged her to give birth to Eros? My advice is to count your blessings, and repair to your own home—your own homes, people. No, you insist on ordering a bowl of oyster stew ($5.90)? Well, now you've done it, you've gone and requested a big bowl of butterfat-greasy white liquid that tastes like fishy milk with some oysters and parsley. If this sends you fleeing to the menu of nonraw, nonfried entrées, I'm betting your night is over, as your fight-or-flight instincts will quickly override your reproductive ones: A fillet of tombo (the Hawaiian name for albacore tuna, $16.40) was so overcooked it flaked like chipboard, and the buttery pink-peppercorn-and-grapefruit-section sauce that accompanied it so unbalanced, so sweet, and so bitter it made my eyes cross. The asparagus that came with the tombo was fine, but the other accompaniment was like somebody's leftover takeout; a molded dome of rice that had sat out, presumably under heat lamps, for so long it had developed a rubbery crust. [...]

There's no refuge in desserts. A berry cobbler ($5.95) was completely liquid: hot jam soup. Chocolate cake ($6.25) was so lacking in chocolate flavor it reminded me of a box-mix cake. Other desserts were just as bad. It's enough to drive a girl to drink.

Dara Moskowitz on *McCormick & Schmick's Seafood Restaurant*, Minneapolis, in *City Pages*, 5 July 2000

Clams: I feel a mild horror about what goes on in the wet darkness between the shells of all bivalves, but clams are the only ones I dislike. Is it their rubbery consistency or their rank subterranean taste, or is the horror deeper than I know?

Jeffrey Steingarten on "My food phobias" in his introduction to *The Man Who Ate Everything* (Alfred A. Knopf, Inc., 1997)

Ma Goa... spits in the face of all that we hold most sacred in these islands by serving up a vindaloo which doesn't require a jeroboam of lager to quell it, which doesn't cause duodenal mayhem. This is one for little Portillo—a great British institution is being wrecked... I look forward to being banged up by little Portillo's taste janitors.

Jonathan Meades on *Ma Goa* in Putney, South West London, in the *Times Saturday Review*, 5 February 1994

One of the sauces which serve the French in place of a state religion.

Ambrose Bierce on mayonnaise

Conran complacency shines through at this noisy and cavernous Soho tourist-trap; surly service and slapdash cooking too often make it a waste of time and money.

Report on *Mezzo*, Harden's London Restaurants 2002

Nothing but joints, joints, joints; sometimes, perhaps, a meat-pie, which, if you eat it, weighs upon your conscience, with the idea that you have eaten the scraps of other people's dinners.

Nathaniel Hawthorne on the fare served up in English hotels.

What, may I ask (and I propose to) do you [experts] know of East Essex as a wine-growing district and of Stoke-by-Gurney in particular?

Since the odds are strongly on your appalling ignorance, here are a few pointers which will enable you to appear as a man of proper savoir faire anywhere between Ducktail Marsh and Pots Islands...

Château Post Office: A very interesting carrot wine, prepared by Miss Foster herself, always in considerable social demand. Somewhat dry to the palate and improved, it is often said, by the addition of brown sugar. The '52s and '54s are still favoured. Beware bottles with little knobbly bits in them.

Clos des Methodists: A unique wine of near-Burgundian nature, though with a blackberry and sloe foundation. High alcoholic content. Only one year ('53) is known, the formula thereafter having been either abandoned or lost by the Minister in Charge. Specimens are rare and highly prized. Decant before serving and leave in the open air.

Wicked Old Wheat Wine (Jackson's elixir): A powerful vin du pays greatly favoured at all local functions. Light in colour and generally dry. Mr. Jackson, grandson of the original vintner, maintains that all years are alike, but the wine matures in the bottle and the older are the more perilous. When opened should be kept away from naked lights.

Hospice de Cyclists' Rest: A stimulating claret-style cordial, raspberry based. Distilled from a recipe in Quiet Moments (1881) with private amendments by Mrs. Bracknell. Beware of the '54s and '55s, an experimental period, and reject all cloudy bottles. Reputed therapeutic value to sufferers from varicose veins. Vintages pre- '53 will remove warts.

Châteauneuf-du-Council (Clos Rampole): A fortified wine of the turnip and mangel type prepared under the personal supervision of Jas Rampole pere et fils. The '56s and '57s, still in cask, enjoy a powerful reputation in the area and are expected to improve in bottle. Connoisseurs are strongly advised to bring their own since the full flavour has on occasion been impaired by vessels previously containing turpentine or oil of cloves.

Le Plonque des Soeurs Forsedyke (1er Cru): A highly reputed wine of semi-sparkling nature, mainly ruby in colour but extremely variable. It is produced at the Villa Holmleigh from available fruits on the augmented infusion principle. The inexperienced are warned against treating this wine as anything but a liqueur. However, Les Soeurs Forsedyke, the proprietors, having been nursing sisters in several campaigns, will accept patients for their "special ward for private friends." On no account touch the '47, which has been described as "unfortunate."

Extract from "A Field for Research" by George Gulley, which appeared in *The Compleat Imbiber* (Putnam, 1958)

⚜

This was a good dinner enough, to be sure; but it was not a dinner to ask a man to.

Samuel Johnson

⚜

The view of Tower Bridge is lovely, but that just can't make up for the uninspiring cooking and sometimes "horrible" service at this perenially dismal Conran group pizzeria.

Report on *Cantina del Ponte*, Harden's London Restaurants 2001

⚜

The Boy's First Pint was about as close as middle-class, middle-century, middle England ever got to the bar mitzvah.

Jonathan Meades on beer, in the *Times Saturday Review*, 8 January 1994

You do get "beautiful people" in the dining room of Ian Schrager's Theatreland design-hotel, but the place is really let down by its wacky fusion menu and by disinterested staff who seem to be paid by the frown.

Report on *Asia de Cuba*, Harden's London Restaurants 2002

Heaven sends us good meat, but the Devil sends cooks.

David Garrick, *On Doctor Goldsmith's Characteristical Cookery* (1777)

The *Cantina del Ponte* is post-Soho Italian, Conran Italian, fashionable Italian. It is surely the loudest of the Peptic Magnate's many enterprises; evidently people who yell for a living on the floor of City exchanges need to keep their instrument in trim after work.

Jonathan Meades on *Cantina del Ponte*, London SE1, in *The Times*, 17 September 1994

"Turbot, Sir," said the waiter, placing before me two fishbones, two eyeballs, and a bit of black mackintosh.

Thomas Earle Welby, in *The Dinner Knell* (1932), "Birmingham or Crewe?"

In order of horribleness: dreary bread, a canapé of duck rilletes that would have been at home on British Airways, and a bellini that tasted of soap and wasn't cold (and then I had to face the empty, dirty glasses for ever until a waiter took one away, leaving the other for ages more). The table was so small the plate of the person opposite (very famous, but I won't give you the name) nearly touched mine. The freebie starter—tomato bavarois, cucumber and tapenade croutonne—was bland and the sauce tasted of mass-produced ketchup. My first course of salmon was okay, no more, and Vanessa's of eggs in a sauce and pastry was actively nasty, the pastry being soggy and tasteless... In order to have the honour of eating this rubbish I had been instructed not to wear jeans. This is one of only two 3-star Michelin restaurants in England, and the menu says "Discover the delights of these exceptional dishes" (always suspect). What is Michel Roux's excuse for serving this quality of food?

Michael Winner on the *Waterside Inn*, Berkshire – "most disappointing restaurant in the UK." From *Winner's Dinners* (Robson Books, 2000)

We had a miserable Trout that made us think of a sickness among the fishes—cheese soup (the only thing which in our travels I turned from in disgust), bad bread, bad butter, indifferent cheese, sorry peaches, and poor wine: and for this fare, the Landlord has the audacity to demand five francs each person.

Dorothy Wordsworth

Yes, it's a disaster!; with its sub-standard comfort food, its indifferent service, and zero atmosphere, MPW's subterranean brasserie, near Piccadilly Circus, strikes many reporters as little short of "shocking."

Report on *Titanic*, Harden's London Restaurants 2002

Duck magret, a cut which has become a cliché—and which often isn't magret (the fattened breast of a foie gras bird) but something puny in an A cup.

Jonathan Meades in the *Times Saturday Review*,
12 March 1994

For the uninitiated, lutefisk is "salt cod"—cod gutted, salted, and dried in the sun, rehydrated with lye, and rinsed with water. The process creates a yellow, mucousy, glob that's trimmed with cream sauce or butter. It tastes foul, like ancient cold creams—slightly salty, with a chemical tinge, and an overpowering odor. But that didn't seem to stop the feeding frenzy.

Dara Moskowitz, restaurant and wine critic for
Minneapolis alternative weekly, City Pages, 9 June 1996

The English are not very dainty; and the greatest Lords' tables, who do not keep French cooks, are covered only with large dishes of meat: they are strangers to bisks and pottage; only once I saw some milk-pottage in a large and deep dish, some of which, as a singular favour, the master of the house gave in a china dish to some of his guests. Their pastry is course and ill-baked; their stewed fruits and confectionery ware cannot be eat; they scarce ever make use of forks or ewers, for they wash their hands by dipping them into a basin of water.

Samuel Sorbiere (d. 1670)

John Dory is the Eurotrash of fish: It boasts an old name but has little to show for it. Surround paupiettes of this tender but bland whitefish with daubs of foie gras and topazlike chunks of chanterelles, however, then splash it about in a brisk, spicy sherry reduction, and you could be convinced the line might be worth saving for future generations.

Hal Rubenstein in *New York Magazine*, 11 September 2000

SaintM (RIP)—the brasserie-style operation at this Covent Garden design-hotel—soon rightly perished; its bizarre, share-a-plate successor, however, continues some of its key features—most notably cardiac arrest on arrival of the bill.

Report on *Tuscan Steak*, Harden's London Restaurants 2002

True sushi connoisseurs are to normal snooty food types what Trappist monks are to the cardinals of Rome. They eat their uncooked fish with a quiet, almost monastic rigor, and their palates are gauged to the tiniest affront...*Jewel Bako* is a restaurant conceived for the most precious kind of sushi aesthete, and if you don't like it, you can take your limp noris and cat-food-filled California rolls and dine someplace else...

Adam Platt on *Jewel Bako* in *New York Magazine*, 16 July 2001

The food was totally beyond human belief. It made British Airways look like Nico Ladenis (my favourite of the three-star British cooks). The croissant was cold and rubbery, there were harmless cornflakes in a plastic container; the cutlery was a new low and I nicked a fork to remind myself of this later. Then I tried a rubbery chocolate brioche thing, followed by what the menu called a "traditional hot breakfast..." When I say unbelievable, I mean unbelievable! I cannot remember anything worse ever being placed before me in my entire life.

> **Michael Winner** on breakfast on the Eurostar train.
> From *Winner's Dinners* (Robson Books, 2000)

Some say it has "great atmosphere, if you're a fan," but, from the majority of reporters the message is "Ref please call time" on this "horrific" West End theme diner, which manages to achieve "awful" standards of everything.

Report on *Football Football*,
Harden's London Restaurants 1999.

⁕⸻⁕

The more intrepid type of traveller cannot blame, and should indeed commend, a primitive community for its inability to produce a whisky and soda when he arrives in its midst with his tongue hanging out. But a whisky and soda is what the intrepid traveller urgently needs. What is he going to do about it?

If we omit suicide, the coward's way out, three courses are open to him.

He goes without.

He has brought plenty of whisky with him.

He settles for a draught of ping, the local spirit, said to be distilled from shredded tamarisk bark.

[...] There are two types of ping: the delayed action and the direct hit. The latter is the less deleterious. Liquor of which a tentative swig produces upon the consumer the illusion that his tongue has been carbonised, brings tears to his eyes and causes him to reel backwards with a stifled imprecation, is liquor that he will thenceforth treat with respect. His mind will quickly get to work fabricating old English proverbs, religious tenets and recent illnesses under cover of which he hopes to escape being plied too assiduously with this firewater; and if in the end he is carried senseless to his tent he will have only himself to blame.

The delayed-action varieties of ping are more insidious. As he quaffs his first bowl of the seemingly innocuous fluid the traveller feels at once relieved and slightly disappointed. 'There's nothing to this stuff,' he tells himself; he beams politely at his hosts and drinks without misgiving the numerous toasts which these friendly fellows gleefully propose.

Before long he is making them a witty speech, partly, for some reason which he does not quite understand, in French. Then, just as he is wondering why it took him so long to notice that each of these splendid chaps has two heads, there is a roaring sound in his ears, and he falls to the ground as though pole-axed, twitching and frothing slightly at the lips.

Extract from *Uncivilised Drinking*, by Peter Fleming, which appeared in *The Compleat Imbiber* (Putnam, 1958)

"Surely it must be illegal to be this bad"—Mezzo's upstairs doles out "inadquate" and "overpriced" oriental fare in cramped refectory conditions.

Report on *Mezzonine*, Harden's London Restaurants 1999

"How would you like your egg? Easy over, hard over, sunny side up…?"
"I'd like it well cooked."
"Sure, but how would you like it cooked? Easy over, hard over, sunny side up?"
It's only breakfast, and I'm already bewildered.

Keith Floyd in *Floyd's American Pie* (BBC Books, 1989)

For my third visit I busted out a wig, spent an hour coming up with different makeup, arrived in a different car with new escorts, and got for my troubles the worst meal yet. …The lobster salad ($18) was again everything I remembered, but the lovefest crashed into a wall with the awful piedina. …Once this dish was like a slow succession of chimes, each note distinct. Now it's like cymbals falling off a bench.

The polenta-mascarpone ravioli ($11.50) were served in a butter sauce, and were so rich they quickly became sickening. They were topped with fresh-shelled peas that were mealy and tasted old. Agnolotti (a ravioli-like pasta, $12.50) had a subtle lamb filling, but there was such a lot of fresh marjoram in the charred tomato sauce that it tasted soapy. A beef filet ($32) tasted red-winey but otherwise undeveloped, though the bed of barley it came on, topped with smoked shallots, was quite good.

After that, I'm not sure whether the tuna or the chicken was worse: It was sort of a fight to the death.

Dara Moskowitz on *D'Amico Cucina*, Minneapolis, in *City Pages*, 27 June 2001

Better named Terminal; with its bland food and slow and sloppy service this run-of-the-mill new City bar/brasserie is "just another Conran...but worse."

Report on *Terminus*, Harden's London Restaurants 2001

The feast consisted of dogs, poultry, pigs, etc.,luäued; that is, after being carefully wrapped in leaves of the ti plant, cooked by being buried amidst stones heated for the purpose...

Near my place at table was a fine young dog luäued, the flesh of which was declared to be excellent by all who partook of it. To my palate, its taste was what I can imagine would result from mingling the flavour of pig and lamb; and I did not hesitate to make my dinner of it, in spite of some qualms at the first mouthful. I must confess when I reflected that the puppy now trussed up before us might have been the affectionate and frolicsome companion of some Hawaiian fair—they all have pet pigs or puppies—I felt as if dog-eating was only a low grade of cannibalism.

W. S. W. Ruschenberger (c. 1836)

The carnal is here unmitigated. The palates of ladies who lunch are not taken into account, which could be a mistake: this is not food for pushing around the plate. Veal tartare is a new one on me and seems about as gastronomically incorrect as you can get.

Jonathan Meades on *Stephen Bull's,*
Fulham Road, London SW3, in
The Times, 16 April 1994

❦

Standards are sinking faster than the Titanic at this cavernous basement, near Piccadilly Circus; the place may offer "a great night out, if you're after a party" (with "lots of beautiful people about"), but, if you want to eat, then the "evil" food and "snotty and disinterested" service are major drawbacks.

Report on *Atlantic Bar & Grill,*
Harden's London Restaurants 1999

❦

It's a tradition as tired as Sparks's décor that steakhouses subliminally punish people who order anything but red meat. How refreshing would it be to end that tradition in a room as newly charged as *Del Frisco's*. When a kitchen is also capable of turning out a deliciously succulent veal porterhouse, a solid, spunky crab cake, osso buco in a becomingly sweet broth with a feisty splash of turtle soup, why must simple dishes like salads feel tossed off, or shrimp rémoulade be flat and rote? Onion rings are a sloppy delight, and skillet potatoes with onions could be a hit at the multiplex, but fried oysters are muddy as the earth in Gladiator, angel's-hair pasta won't even twirl on a fork, and the spinach is hardly—as its name claims—"supreme." Every fish is okay, no more, no less. But what's not okay—in fact, it's infuriating—is the unfulfilling, furiously hawked 30-ounce lobster tail that thrashed Cleveland. For $136 you get to struggle with a dead sea creature. For almost that much, you could swim with a porpoise.

Hal Rubenstein on *Del Frisco's* in
New York Magazine, 5 June 2000

It may offer a people-watching extravaganza, but the dining room of Ian Schrager's north-of-Oxford-Street design hotel is an extremely pretentious place, with a daft menu and crazy prices.

Report on *Spoon+*, Harden's London Restaurants 2002

After this horrible main course was cleared away, the desserts were fine. Except for my American producer's. He ordered cheese and biscuits. Now to serve cheese and biscuits you do not need an advanced degree in culinary art. All you need is some cheese and some biscuits and the strength to bring them to the table at more or less the same time. This was too much for the Bibendum waiter. He managed the cheese all right. Then he went and stood next to the biscuits sitting on a serving area nearby. He stood, and stood. My American friend, after a long wait because he was one of those quiet, far too polite Americans, said: "I did ask for biscuits." At that point my frustration boiled over, and I gave the waiter speech 24A. Biscuits appeared with total regularity, after that.

Michael Winner on *Bibendum*, Fulham Road, London.
From *Winner's Dinners* (Robson Books, 2000)

The Greeks are really good at both pre-Socratic philosophy and white statues. They have not been good cooks since the fifth century BC, when Siracusa on Sicily was the gastronomic capital of the world. Typical of modern-day Greek cuisine are feta cheese

and retsina wine. Any country that pickles its national cheese in
brine and adulterates its national wine with pine pitch should
order dinner at the local Chinese place and save its energies for
other things.

Jeffrey Steingarten, "My food phobias," in his introduction to
The Man Who Ate Everything (Alfred A. Knopf, Inc., 1997).

"Rubbish food, rubbish service, top-class bill"—even by Conran
standards, the "sterile" dining room of this design-hotel by
Liverpool Street is a plain and simple "rip-off."

Report on *Aurora*, Harden's London Restaurants 2002

There is nothing so vile or repugnant to nature, but you may
please prescription for it, in the customs of some nation or other.
A Parisian likes mortified flesh; a native of Legiboli will not taste
his fish till it is quite putrified; the civilized inhabitants of
Kamschatka get drunk with the urine of their guests, whom they
have already intoxicated; the Nova-Zemblans make merry on
train-oil; the Groenlanders eat in the same dish with their dogs;
the Caffres, at the Cape of Good Hope, piss upon those whom
they delight to honour, and feast upon a sheep's intestines with
their contents, as the greatest dainty that can be presented. A
true-bred Frenchman dips his fingers, imbrowned with snuff, into
his plate filled with ragout.

Tobias Smollett

"Coleslaw or salad?"
"Salad, please."
"What kinda dressing? Blue Cheese, Thousand Island, Ranch,
French, Italian, Creamy Italian…?"

"Blue Cheese, please. And some beer."
"Bud, Bud Light, Coors, Michelob, Michelob Light…?"
Here we go again.

Keith Floyd in *Floyd's American Pie* (BBC Books, 1989)

It was a legendary place to belong before you ever thought you knew where you were supposed to go. Before everyone began craving tapas and tirami su, or ever heard of a fruit named in honor of passion; before the pilgrimage of Jews to Chinatown for what they unknowingly called "chinks"; before outsiders realized that Le Cirque's famed pasta primavera wasn't actually on the menu; before Ian Fleming's revelatory declaration of "shaken, not stirred," *21* beckoned with curved red banquettes, steak tartare, and martinis as breathtakingly dry as George Sanders's putdowns of Anne Baxter between bites at a table there in *All About Eve*. Going to Paris for the weekend was never "hot." It was just something you wanted to do at least once before you died. Like boarding the Orient Express. Like throwing three coins in the Fountain of Trevi. Like lunching at *21* […]

Then you bite down, and it's like Invasion of the Flavor Snatchers. Granted, the filet is its least gamy cut, but how can venison taste just like lamb, whose flavor is almost identical to the rabbit, which could have fooled us as chicken except that the wood-fired organic bird is even paler. Bass, snapper, swordfish— all indistinguishable except for the overcooked accompaniments. Is there no spice rack in the kitchen? No marinade? Garlic, lemon, salt? Ketchup, even? Nothing going on with the shrimp, nothing at all. Caesar salad is fair, but so is Soup Burg's. The game broth is like College Inn low-sodium broth. Everyone stares at the "classic Senegalese" soup because no one believes it really isn't cold milk and parsley. Grilled rib-eye creates a bit of spark, but only because it actually has a passing scent of steak. Pork chops are impenetrable, though the apple-cidered yams are great. We hate to do this to Jean, so we spit out the chicken hash when he isn't looking. Adding up how many Big Macs you could buy for one $24 21 burger isn't fair.

Hal Rubenstein on *21* in *New York Magazine*,
9 February 1998

"Disastrous" West End theme-diner; let's hope that, like all fashions, this "nightmare"—"a simply awful experience in all regards"—passes very soon.

Report on *Fashion Cafe*, Harden's London Restaurants 1999

The business of restaurant reviewing comes with all sorts of salutary benefits. You aren't trapped in an office, for one thing. You are paid to lounge around in elaborate settings while highly trained professionals fawn all over you. You eat for free, and it is your duty (in fact, it is your job) to steal food off other people's plates. But if you're an obsessive eater, like me, there's also a darker, more Faustian side to this bargain… *D'Artagnan*, run by the partners who own the foie gras purveyor of the same name, has a menu consisting largely of…foie gras. *Artisanal* is the chic new Park Avenue fromagerie devoted to the fast-growing cult of cheese. I asked my wife to accompany me on this cholesterol odyssey, but after one visit to *Artisanal*, she diplomatically took to her bed with a cold. My father, a diplomat by training, was less diplomatic. "My gosh," he said, "that sounds like a near-death experience to me."

Adam Platt on *Artisanal and D'Artagnan* in
New York Magazine, 28 May 2001

Though this "continually disappointing" faux-French chain has its supporters, we're 100% behind those who find it "quite simply dreadful in every way."

Report on *Cafe Rouge*, Harden's London Restaurants 1998

❦

The menu at the *Café du Jardin* translates poulet provençal as "brick flattened chicken," which sounds like a terrible thing to have happened to a fowl—the result of a tragic hod incident on La Canebiere, perhaps.

This is not the only solecism on show. The two doors to the street are constantly left open, causing the customer who has drawn the short seat to get up time and again to fight back the draught. The staff are on the diffident side. The tables are so cramped that intimacy could well occur, Constable.

Jonathan Meades in the
Times Saturday Review, 12 March 1994

❦

Tuesday, 6 December 1870: Today I found on my restaurant bill-of-fare buffalo, antelope, and kangaroo! ...
Thursday, 8 December 1870: I have just been shown some dog cutlets; they look really very good, and might be mutton for all one can see to the contrary...
Saturday, 7 January 1871: The ration of horseflesh, its weight 33 centigrammes, including bone, intended for the consumption of two persons for three days, is merely enough to satisfy the appetite of a normal being at lunch.

Edmond de Goncourt in his journal during the siege of Paris

❦

To chart these trajectories of fashion and taste, sociologists have invented the "diffusion curve." At the bottom of the curve are "innovators," who create the trend, followed by "early adopters," who begin to popularize it… the "laggards"… are the last to co-opt a particular fashion. When there are more laggards at the party than anyone else, the party is officially over.

Virot, which opened a month or so ago on the ground floor of the new Dylan hotel, in midtown, looks like a laggard to me…One delicate foodie aristocrat at our table was shocked to the core when the chanterelles on her otherwise expertly prepared tart turned out to be rancid…The avocado soup was too sludgy to enhance the taste of the crabmeat, and the cromesqui, which should be subtle little beignets, had skins as thick as hushpuppies.

Adam Platt on *Virot* in *New York Magazine*, 30 April 2001

Quite when the Japanese discovered English mustard and bottled brown sauce I'm not sure, but I am sure that Japanese restaurants must be the only places other than grease cafs which now use those coarse condiments. Here, anything that is done in bread-crumbs gets the same treatment—shredded leaves in a dressing that tastes like Sandwich Spread, hot-dog mustard, OK or A1 or Daddy's in a little sauce bowl.

Jonathan Meades on *Musha* in West London in
the *Times Saturday Review*, 5 March 1994

I would always advise those who wish to drink coffee in England, to mention before hand how many cups are to be made with half an ounce; or else the people will probably bring them a prodigious quantity of brown water; which (notwithstanding all my admonitions) I have not yet been able wholly to avoid.

Carl Philipp Moritz

There's the aforementioned non-mentioned moniker, the half-lit doorfront marked by incense, a velvet rope, and a bouncer who served as a temple dog in a prior life.

But enter, and the Forbidden City factor fades faster than you can count blondes in black tank dresses…It's like the most spectacular bowling-alley cocktail lounge ever built. If only they had put in a half dozen lanes downstairs instead of a dance floor…

Hal Rubenstein on hard-to-find *Lotus* in
New York Magazine, 11 September 2000

There I was, withered to my bones with dehydration. Tumbleweeds rattled around in the bone-dry mesa of my water glass. My waiter had apparently given up the profession and lit out for a better life. The floor manager was busy giving free drinks to another, louder table, to apologize to them for all the things they wanted that they couldn't have—like food, and for them wine, since no one thought to entrust the floor manager with the key to the tantalizing wine cellar. It had been a long hour since I placed an appetizer order, and I might as well have been waiting for a bus for all the fine dining I was doing. I felt like Pamela Anderson at a NAMBLA convention. Had I not been a food critic—and in this case, incredibly, dining with another local food critic—I would have wept.

Yet instead, when our waiter, apparently having met disappointment on the coasts, returned at one-hour 10-minutes (sans H2O), and asked, incredibly, whether we needed more bread— well that was merely the beginning of the hilarity. I laughed. When I said no, we had plenty of bread, the waiter, not trusting me— and why should he, with me sneaking into his section and marring a life of vagabond adventure—unwrapped the focaccia in its napkin-nest, peeked in at it, rewrapped it, and strode off again to his lair. I laughed so hard I thought I'd rupture something. Actually, I'm still laughing about it. Because it's not just me getting the worst service in the world: It's me getting the worst service in the world while taking notes. [...] When the young, key-free manager arrived and he identified the little stem-on vegetable as a Japanese eggplant, I couldn't stop giggling. Then I tasted it, and I stopped laughing. It was bitter, charred, and awful—it made me want to spit. (If you ever wondered why people salt and drain eggplants, take a cute little past-prime Japanese eggplant, char it over an open flame, and pop it into your mouth. You'll salt forevermore.)

Dara Moskowitz on *Mpls. Café* in *City Pages*, 15 October 1997

❧

Hell, drinking light beer is like taking a shower with your boots on.

Doug Goodman, quoted by Keith Floyd in *Floyd's American Pie* (BBC Books, 1989)

❧

Adults who require a salad at every meal are like obsessed little children who will eat nothing but frozen pizza or canned ravioli for months on end. They tuck into the dreariest salad simply because it is raw and green. No matter that the arugula is edged with brown, the croutons taste rancid, the vinegar burns like battery acid. No matter that it is the dead of winter when salad chills us to the marrow and we should be eating preserved meats and hearty roots, garbures, and cassoulet. No matter that they are keeping me from my desert. They think nothing of interrupting a perfectly nice meal with their superstitious salad ritual.

Jeffrey Steingarten in *The Man Who Ate Everything* (Alfred A. Knopf, Inc., 1997)

❧

If they had relied on Elizabeth David, who was a collector of recipes rather than a technical instructor, all those chefs who now cook in a manner which is ascribable to her would still be producing the grot that characterised Sixties bistros. They can only do "Elizabeth David" because they have learnt in a more rigorous school, one which places greater emphasis on temperature and precision than it does on, oh, the immemorial marbling of an aubergine's skin in the market in Orange.

Jonathan Meades in the *Times Saturday Review*,
19 February 1994

The bill of fare, he scanned it through
To see what two half-cents would do.
The only item of them all
For two half-cents was one fish ball.
So to the waiter he did call
And gently whispered: "One fish ball."
The waiter bellowed down the hall:
"The gentleman here wants one fish ball."
The diners looked both one and all
To see who wanted one fish ball.
The wretched man, all ill at ease,
Said: "A little bread, sir, if you please."
The waiter bellowed down the hall:
"We don't serve bread with one fish ball."
The wretched man, he felt so small,
He quickly left the dining hall.
The wretched man, he went outside
And shot himself until he died.
This is the moral of it all,
Don't ask for bread with one fish ball.

Anon. Quoted in *The Greedy Book*
compiled by Brian Hill

When we came in we sat down—nobody was come—no table laid—no appearance of dinner. On my life there is nothing so heartless as going out to dinner and finding no dinner ready. I sat down; the company began to drop in—Charles Lamb and his poor sister—all sorts of odd, clever people. Still no dinner. At last came in a maid who laid a cloth and put down knives and forks in a heap. Then followed a dish of potatoes, cold, waxy, and yellow. Then came a great bit of beef with a bone like a battering ram, toppling on all its corners. Neither Hazlitt nor Lamb seemed at all disturbed, but set to work helping each other; while the boy, half-clean and obstinate, kept squalling to put his fingers into the gravy. Even Lamb's wit and Hazlitt's disquisitions, in a large room, wainscotted and ancient, where Milton had meditated, could not reconcile me to such violation of all the decencies of life.

B. R. Haydon on dinner at William Hazlitt's to mark Hazlitt junior's christening

Heaven for wrestling fans, hell for the rest of us, this new multi-screen Times Square themery strikes critics as "cheesy enough to cushion a body slam" with food that "tasted better at XFL games."

Review of WWF, New York, in *Zagat*

Heaven keep every Christian from their gravies, which are made of one-third meal and two-thirds butter, or when a change is needed, one-third butter and two-thirds meal. And Heaven guard everyone from their naïve vegetables which, boiled away in water, are brought to the table just as God made them!

Heinrich Heine on English food

They consume an extraordinary quantity of bacon. Ham and beefsteaks appear morning, noon, and night. In eating, they mix things together with the strangest incongruity imaginable. I have seen eggs and oysters eaten together; the sempiternal ham with apple-sauce; beef-steak with stewed peaches; and salt fish with onions. The bread is everywhere excellent, but they rarely enjoy it themselves, as they insist upon eating horrible half-baked hot rolls both morning and evening.

Frances Trollope on American eating habits of the 1830s

It causeth troublesome dreams, and sends up black vapours to the brain.

Robert Burton on cabbage

The vulgar boil, the learned roast, an egg.

Alexander Pope, *Imitations of Horace* (1738)

I never see an egg brought on my table but I feel penetrated with the wonderful change it would have undergone but for my gluttony; it might have been a gentle useful hen, leading her chickens with a care and vigilance which speaks shame to many women.

St John de Crévecoeur,
Letters from an American Farmer (1782)

Then my stomach must digest its waistcoat.
    Richard Brinsley Sheridan, when told that drinking would
ruin the coat of his stomach; in *Sheridaniana* (1826)

Vindaloo is a great British dish. Lip-smackin', finger-lickin' great, in
fact—although you must remember not to stick the partially
licked finger in your eye unless you're in the mood for ocular
grief. That's one of the things about vindaloo—it hurts. It's the
staple diet of more than 90 per cent of Britain's colonic
masochists.
    The other thing about it is that in certain primitive societies
(Aldershot, Catterick, Larkhill) ingestion of the stuff is reckoned
to be an act of machismo, of extra-manliness—you can't say that
of other great British dishes such as frozen pizza, filthburger, hot
dog with red and yellow mucous, smoky bacons, packet soups.
Vindaloo is more than a food, the way that three six-packs are
more than a drink.
    Jonathan Meades in the *Times Saturday Review*,
5 February 1994

A "great location on the river" helps make this Richmond year-
ling a beautiful spot; it's also "grossly overpriced and pretentious,"
and offers "terrible" south-west American cooking, so its appeal
is pretty much limited to sunny day brunching.
    Report on *Canyon*, Harden's London Restaurants 2001

"You're my prize eaters," our server assured my table one night,
incredulous that we had plowed through two rounds of
appetizers, followed by entrées and sides—and then, perhaps
most incredibly, finished the desserts. I didn't have the heart to

tell him that out of my series of meals at *Red Fish Blue* my over-whelming impression was of dishes, dishes everywhere, but hardly a drop to eat. [...]

Unfortunately, I can also confidently say I've hardly seen such foul paella and bouillabaisse as the stuff served here. Both of these dishes cost $12.95 a person and require a minimum order of two portions. The bouillabaisse was a lukewarm serving of dry, flinty rice in a watery broth that tasted like nothing whatsoever. It was topped with overcooked, rubbery clams, mussels, and shrimp, and came with lots and lots of overcooked green peas(!) and cubes of long-boiled carrot and potato. It seemed like something meant to punish felons. In contrast, the rice in the paella was exactly the opposite...so gummy, runny, and sticky it looked like it had been poured out of a can. It didn't taste any better, and was crowned by mussels and clams that were, again, terribly overcooked and chewy. Burned little nuggets of chorizo lurking in the rice tried to help the situation but could not.

Yes, burned. I was also served calamari ($7.50), burned to an unattractive mahogany and paired with a "horseradish aioli" that tasted like sour cream and horseradish. Hush puppies ($3) were burned at the same meal, and at another lunch the little crab cakes on a crab-cake salad were burned. At a third meal the basket of homemade breads ($5) were re-warmed so violently, they became hard and shriveled. I couldn't even break the Cheddar-and-chive biscuits with my bare hands.

Dara Moskowitz on *Red Fish Blue*, St. Paul, in *City Pages*, 7 February 2001

❦

10 April 1830: I have heard of the King [George IV] this morning. What do you think of His breakfast yesterday morning for an Invalid? A Pidgeon and Beef Steak Pye of which he eat two Pigeons and three Beef-steaks, Three parts of a Bottle of Mozelle, a Glass of Dry Champagne, two Glasses of Port [&] a Glass of

Brandy! He had taken Laudanum the night before, again before this breakfast, again last night and again this morning!

Arthur Wellesley, 1st Duke of Wellington
(the king died on 26 June)

❦

What followed belonged to a markedly lower caste of cooking. It might be suggested that in order to obtain the true Russian flavour it is necessary to employ a heavy hand and cheap lard... Deep-fried courgettes are horrible—this is where the lard comes in; although of course maybe the cooking agent isn't lard but hydrogenated vegetable oil. Whatever it is, it should be abandoned.

Jonathan Meades on *Rasputin*, London NW1, in
The Times, 25 June 1994

❦

Piggery has spawned a glossy bimonthly, *A la Carte*, a gastronomic *Penthouse* devoted to glamour photography, the subject of which is not the female body imaged as if it were good enough to eat, but food photographed according to the conventions of the pin-up. (Barr and Levy, ever quick with a quip, dub this kind of thing "gastro-porn".) The colour plates are of awesome voluptuousness. Oh, that coconut kirsch roulade in the first issue! If, as Lévi-Strauss once opined, "to eat is to fuck," then that coconut kirsch roulade is just asking for it. Even if the true foodie knows there is something not quite... about a coconut kirsch roulade as a concept. It is just a bit... just a bit Streatham. Its vowels are subtly wrong. It is probably related to a Black Forest gâteau.

Angela Carter, in the *London Review of Books*, 1984

❦

Strawberry soup is merely a purée, and at $18.50, a baked Alaska rages on like the finale of Burning Man, only to blacken its meringue while still reeking of alcohol, leaving the ice cream inside hard enough to shatter the patio glass.

Considering its physical enormity and enviable annual gross, it's admirable, even stunning, that *Tavern on the Green* has made such a concerted effort to be taken seriously as a restaurant. But with this tariff, effort isn't enough. A new executive chef has just been announced, but for the time being, that emerald-green chandelier outshines anything on a plate. If this is as far as they can go, at least throw in a monogrammed T-shirt from the gift shop.

> **Hal Rubenstein** on *Tavern on the Green*, Central Park,
> in *New York Magazine*, 24 August 1998

I may only be a poor boy from Willesden, but I don't need some snotty girl telling me it's "in" to serve a plate of food that would satisfy three people as a main dish 2 1/2 hours after dinner has started.

"Do you want anything else?" asked Kelly. "I'd like to go," I replied. I'd also like to be lobotomised, so the evening in *Nobu* is removed from my memory.

> **Michael Winner** on *Nobu*, London.
> From *Winner's Dinners* (Robson Books, 2000).

"Ridiculously smug," "dreadfully overpriced" Mayfair establishment, serving "very boring Italian food, with attitude."

> **Report** on *Cecconi's*, Harden's London Restaurants 1995

The bitter black coffee may have been brewed only once a week. The ham could be dry, salty, and tough. Hard-cooked eggs were stored for an indeterminate period of time in limed water to keep them from discoloring. Fried eggs may have been cooked in rancid grease and certainly were served on stale bread. Here also one found leaden biscuits—their nickname, "sinkers," giving a clue as to their quality—and something which earned the euphemism "railroad pie." The recipe was thought to be to take two crusts of cardboard and fill them with thickened glue.

James D. Porterfield, *Dining by Rail: The History and the Recipes of America's Golden Age of Railroad Cuisine* (New York: St Martin's Press, 1993)

Once, during Prohibition, I was forced to live for days on nothing but food and water.

W. C. Fields

Clams: I simply cannot imagine why anyone would eat something slimy served in an ashtray.

Miss Piggy, *Miss Piggy's Guide to Life*, 1981

Theater

When you've seen all of Ionesco's plays, I felt at the end, you've seen one of them.

Kenneth Tynan after seeing *Victims of Duty*
by Eugène Ionesco, 1960

⚜

The first rule for a young playwright to follow is not to write like Henry Arthur Jones… The second and third rules are the same.

Oscar Wilde

⚜

There is less in this than meets the eye.

Comment by Tallulah Bankhead to Alexander Woollcott
while watching a revival of Maeterlinck's
Aglavine and Selysette

⚜

Is it a stale remark to say that I have constantly found the interest excited at a playhouse to bear an exact inverse proportion to the price paid for the admission?

Charles Lamb on the theater

⚜

She has offered us…pleasant enough but wholly unimportant performances of unimportant roles in such unimportant plays as *The Enchanted Cottage* (that dish of mush by Pinero out of Barrie), *The Outsider* (that geyser of hokum), *Casanova* (that couturière's parade), *The Way Things Happen* (that Owen Davis exhibit written by an Englishwoman), *The Age of Innocence* (that box-office pat on grandma's back) and *Alien Corn* (that that)…

George Jean Nathan on the
actress Katherine Cornell

⚘

You know, I go to the theatre to be entertained…I don't want to see plays about rape, sodomy, and drug addiction…I can get all that at home.

Peter Cooke, *The Observer*, caption to cartoon, 8 July 1962

⚘

Mr. Clarke played the King all evening as though under constant fear that someone else was about to play the Ace.

Eugene Field of the *Denver Post*, referring to
Creston Clarke's performance of *King Lear*

⚘

Ladies…just a little more virginity, if you don't mind.

Sir Herbert Beerbohm Tree to the female extras in a
New York production of *Henry VIII*

⚘

On the whole, I would advise you to read the play rather than to see it. One can skip a book without troubling any one, whereas it is selfish to dodge in and out of a theatre where the mimes are doing their best and most of the audience is anxious to take out its money's-worth in attention.

Max Beerbohm on *Pygmalion*, 16 June 1900

Funny without being vulgar.

Sir William Swenk Gilbert —of Gilbert and Sullivan fame— referring to Sir Henry Irving's *Hamlet* (attrib.)

Long experience has taught me that in Britain nobody goes to the theatre unless he or she has bronchitis.

James Agate, *Ego 6*

To the King's Theatre, where we saw *Midsummer's Night's Dream*, which I have never seen before, nor shall ever again, for it is the most insipid, ridiculous play that ever I saw in my life.

Samuel Pepys in his diary, 29 September 1662

We were as nearly bored as enthusiasm would permit.

Sir Edmund Gosse, referring to a play by Swinburne

All my envy goes to the inspired Mr. Walter Winchell, who walked wanly out into the foyer after the third act—there are four acts and they are long, long acts—and summed up the whole thing in the phrase, "Well, for Crichton out loud!"

Dorothy Parker, reviewing the Broadway opening of *The Admirable Crichton* by J. M. Barrie for *The New Yorker*

The real complexity of life among Mr. Lonsdale's powerfully sexed grammarians can be indicated in a sentence, though a tough one: Michael, engaged to Molly, is really in love with Diana, whom he seduced once in Paris; George can't decide whether to marry Celia or Maggie, both of whom he has seduced here and there at various times; and Elsie, though married to Reggie, is still strongly attracted to her first husband, John, who has seduced practically everybody and likes to talk about it. Anyway, all these people, along with a drunken butler and an old family lawyer, both standard models, are visible on the stage, sometimes all at once.

Wolcott Gibbs on *Another Love Story* by Frederick Lonsdale, from *Season in the Sun & Other Pleasures* (Random House, 1946)

Satire is what closes on Saturday night.

George S. Kaufman

The Cigarette Girl certainly made me gasp in amazement, it is so unbelievably bad...The dialogue is putrid, the acting early marionette, the evening disastrous.

Review in the *Daily Mirror*, June 1962

I have been looking around for an appropriate wooden gift and am pleased hereby to present you with Elsi Ferguson's performance in her new play.

Alexander Woollcott in a telegram to George and Bea Kaufman on the occasion of their fifth wedding anniversary; recorded in *George S. Kaufman and the Algonquin Round Table* by Scott Meredith

This vaudeville humor Mr. Coward cleverly brings the less humorously penetrating to accept as wit by removing its baggy pants and red undershirt and dressing it up in drawing-room style. But it remains vaudeville humor just the same.

George Jean Nathan, on Noël Coward

⚜

... Vera bad.

Punch review of Oscar Wilde's play *Vera or The Nihilists*,
1 September 1883

⚜

The costumes are by Balmain, and Christopher Renshaw directed the slow-moving traffic.

Charles Osborne's final thoughts on *Paris Match* by
Jean Poiret. From *First Nights, Second Thoughts*
(Bellew Publishing, 2001)

⚜

I have tried lately to read Shakespeare, and found it so intolerably dull that it nauseated me.

Charles Darwin on William Shakespeare,
Autobiography

⚜

All persons of thought will confess to no great fondness for acting which particularly seeks to "tickle the ears of the groundlings." We allude to the loud mouthed ranting style which is much the ambition of some of our players, particularly the younger ones. They take every occasion, in season and out of season, to try the extremist strength of their lungs. If they have to enact passion they do so by all kinds of violent and unnatural

jerks, swings, screwing of the nerves of the face, rolling of the eyes, and so on. To men of taste, all this is exceedingly ridiculous.
Walt Whitman, in the *Brooklyn Eagle*, 1846

※❀❀※

This is M. Ionesco's first attempt at a social play, and the number of interpretations to which it is susceptible is roughly equal to the number of people in the audience.
Kenneth Tynan on *Rhinoceros* by Eugène Ionesco, 1960

※❀❀※

...she settles for a number of unsubtle readings. When Lövborg and Mrs. Elvsted are about to seat themselves, Hedda says coyly. "I want to sit between you," with all the subtlety of a truck.
Stanley Kauffmann reviewing Claire Bloom as Hedda in
Hedda Gabler, Playhouse, New York, March 1971

※❀❀※

The essence of this play is wit, and there is not power either in Nature or outside it to make wit endurable to the English playgoer...
This piece is so witty and wise, so completely suited to the grown-up mind, and so full of theatre as the French understand theatre, both in high comedy and in Palais-Royal farce, that in my opinion it is doomed to failure.
James Agate, in the *Sunday Times*, reviewing
Reunion in Vienna by Robert E. Sherwood, 1933

※❀❀※

Richard Whorf and José Ferrer made *Volpone* into a kind of raucous collegiate romp, more reminiscent of a Marx Brothers film than of that terrible Noah's Ark of carnivora that Jonson, master-carpenter, beached on the English stage.

Mary McCarthy's review of *Volpone*, by Ben Jonson, April 1948

Hamlet is often demoniacal; Mr. Forbes Robertson, as an actor, has very little demon in him. He speaks the philosophical pieces in a conventional mode, without much conviction, and they are numerous. [...] He showed signs at first (but repressed them) of using a suggestive kind of hysterical pantomime which might be thought to foreshow Hamlet's madness.

Oliver Elton reviewing *Hamlet* for
The Manchester Guardian, 23 May 1898

Miss Strozzi... had the temerity to wear as truly horrible a gown as ever I have seen on the American stage. There was a flowing skirt of pale chiffon—you men don't have to listen—and a bodice of rose-coloured taffeta, the sleeves of which ended shortly below her shoulders. Then there was an expanse of naked arms, and then, around the wrists, taffeta frills such as are fastened about the unfortunate necks of beaten white poodle-dogs in animal acts. Had she not luckily been strangled by a member of the cast while disporting this garment, I should have fought my way to the stage and done her in myself.

Dorothy Parker, writing in *The New Yorker*, on
Kay Strozzi in *The Silent Witness*, 1931

Mr. Robinson was game, all right. But what is gameness in a man who is suffering from delusions of adequacy?

Walter Kerr on Jay Robinson's performance
in *Buy Me Blue*

Charles Darnton, in *The Evening World*, described *The Easiest Way* as "an evening of good acting and bad morals." Personally, I prefer that to an evening of good morals and bad acting. It is the combination of bad morals, bad play, and bad playing which I should like to see left to Archbishop Farley and Manager Burnham.

Channing Pollock on *The Easiest Way* (by Eugene Walter) in *The Green Book Album*, April 1909.

To the Duke's house, and there saw *Twelfth-Night* acted well, though it be but a silly play, and not relating at all to the name or day.

Samuel Pepys in his Diary, 6 January 1663

How beautiful it would be for someone who could not read.

G. K. Chesterton (attrib.), referring to the lights on Broadway

---

Having closely compared Peter Brooke's production of *Titus Andronicus* with Peter Hall's production of *Cymbeline*, I am persuaded that these two young directors should go at once into partnership. I have even worked out business cards for them:

Hall & Brook, Ltd, the Home of Lost Theatrical Causes. Collapsing plays shored up, unspeakable lines glossed over, unactable scenes made bearable. Wrecks salvaged, ruins refurbished: unpopular plays at popular prices. Masterpieces dealt with only if neglected. Shakespearean juvenilia and senilia our speciality: if it can walk, we'll make it run. Bad last acts no obstacle: if it peters out, call Peter in. Don't be fobbed off with Glenvilles, Woods, or Zadeks: look for the trademark—Hall & Brook.

Kenneth Tynan, 1957

As (the) husband who sacrifices his faith for worldly gain, Charlton Heston, a pretty fellow whom the moving pictures should exultantly capture without delay, if they have any respect for the dramatic stage, duly adjusts his chemise so the audience may swoon over his expansive, hirsute chest and conducts his prize physique about the platform like a physical culture demonstrator.

George Jean Nathan. Charlton Heston was appearing in
Design for a Stained Glass Window, Mansfield Theater,
January 1950

Farley Granger played Mr. Darcy with all the flexibility of a telegraph pole.

Brooks Atkinson reviewing a musical version of
Pride and Prejudice by Bo Goldman, on Broadway in the 1950s

One has the illusion of watching Camille played by a small town high-school girl. This is part of an abiding immaturity which one finds difficult to describe in such words as will distinguish it from arrested development.

Alexander Woollcott on Lilian Gish in *Camille*
in *The New Yorker*, 1932

Mr. H. Brooke's King was not positively bad, but we had hoped that it would be more positively good.

W. T. Arnold reviewing *Hamlet* for
The Manchester Guardian, 22 November 1882

An eight-year-old youngster who glories in the melodramatic name Brandon de Wilde is amusing as the little pest whose monkeyshines bedevil the two principal characters and would doubtless be even more so if one could always make out what he was saying. From where I sat, much of what he mouthed sounded as if it were something out of a modern version of *Prometheus Unbound* by James Joyce.

George Jean Nathan on de Wilde, then a child actor, in *The Member of the Wedding* by Carson McCullers, January 1950

ↁ⊛ↀ

In fact, now that you've got me right down to it, the only thing I didn't like about *The Barretts of Wimpole Street* was the play.

Dorothy Parker in *The New Yorker*, 1931

ↁ⊛ↀ

On its face value, it is callous and empty enough: what lies in its Freudian depths one dreads to think.

Anthony Seymour in the *Yorkshire Post* on Harold Pinter's *The Homecoming*, June 1965

ↁ⊛ↀ

It is alleged that one of the most deplorable aspects of contemporary play-reviewing is its habit of either condemning a presentation outright and with no modifications or eulogizing it to the skies, also with no modifications. Something, in short, is either totally excellent or totally awful. By way of giving further support to the allegation, which hasn't much basis in fact, let me say, with no reservations, whatever, that this farce-comedy of Mr. Young's is totally awful.

George Jean Nathan reviewing *Ask my Friend Sandy* by Stanley Young, February 1943

211

The progress is very slow. It might almost be described as uneventful, since all the chief marvels of the play happen "off", and are known by us only at second-hand. True, Mr. Strange's stage-directions provide for the burning of Rome before our very eyes. But the London County Council, more zealous for our safety than for our delight, does not permit real holocausts on any stage. Consequently, Nero's fiddling is accompanied by nothing more awesome than some pink magnesian light behind transparent back-cloths.

Max Beerbohm, 12 May 1900

An audience goes to the theatre to sit for an hour or so, not for a day. Mr. O'Neill seems to think that time is a negligible element in the development of his ideas.

Comment by a member of the audience on
Beyond the Horizon by Eugene O'Neill, November 1920

It has very little to do with birds and a great deal to do with glib mystic episode and spurious spiritual insight…At the start, a drink—tea, I suppose—is brewed on stage, then poured into two big bowls that are passed around to be shared by the audience. (Sitting in the back, I missed my sip.) At the end the narrator asked the audience to come up and join hands with the company in a large circle. Dozens did. I left, shocked by this Julian Beck-Judith Malina cheapness in a Brook group. Perhaps they are all still standing there, locked in a new community…

Stanley Kauffmann on *The Conference of Birds*, performed by
Peter Brook's group from the International Centre for Theatre
Research in Paris, Brooklyn Academy of Music, October 1973

My dearest dread is in the word "yesterday" in the name of a play; for I know that sometime during the evening I am going to be transported, albeit kicking and screaming, back to the scenes and the costumes of a tenderer time. And I know, who show these scars to you, what the writing and the acting of those episodes of tenderer times are going to be like. I was not wrong, heaven help me, in my prevision of the Milne work. Its hero is caused, by a novel device, to fall asleep and a-dream; and thus he is given yesterday. Me, I should have given him twenty years to life.

Dorothy Parker on *Give Me Yesterday* by A. A. Milne, in *The New Yorker*, 1931

Gielgud himself is quite simply over-parted. In his hands Othello dwindles into a coffee-stained Leontes; instead of a wounded bull, dangerous despite its injuries, we have an heraldic eagle with its wings harmlessly clipped. From some of the quieter passages ("Here is my journey's end," for example), Sir John extracts a wonderful music of resignation; but his voice has no body, no nakedness, no explosive power, and few more blatant falsehoods have ever been uttered on the English stage than when this Othello declares that he lacks "those soft parts of conversation that chamberers have."

Kenneth Tynan on Franco Zeffirelli's 1961 production of *Othello*, at Stratford-on-Avon, with John Gielgud in the title role.

At the beginning of Hamlet the stage looks like a Build-Your-Own-Elsinore kit.

Robert Cushman in the *Observer*, 1981

The Life and Times of Joseph Stalin...was announced to run from 7pm to 7am. I don't usually review productions I haven't seen completely—I'm told Stalin actually ran until 9am and 100 people sat through it all—but I would like to comment on the two and a half hours that I saw...Two points are immediately clear: narrative is not the object; and the title, despite the photo, is irrelevant to anything I saw. (I'm told that, some hours after dawn, there were specific references to Stalin.)

Stanley Kauffmann reviewing a play produced by Robert Wilson at the Brooklyn Academy of Music, 1974

Superb and inimitable as it all is, it is mostly an objective and physiological kind of beauty the soul finds in Shakspere (sic)—a style supremely grand of the sort, but in my opinion stopping short of the grandest sort, at any rate for fulfilling and satisfying modern and scientific and democratic American purposes.

Walt Whitman on Shakespeare, in *November Boughs*

The King will be better when Mr. Francis Sullivan plays him outside his robes instead of in them and the Queen of Miss Dorothy Dix conveys the impression of not being in the play at all, but of looking in now and again to do a bit of acting. As Ophelia, Miss Cherry Cotterell strikes me as being unripe. Mr. Torin Thatcher makes an inaudible ghost and Mr. Frederick Bennett's First Gravedigger is the one gloomy spot in the entire production.

James Agate on Tyrone Guthrie's production of *Hamlet* at the Old Vic, January 1937

Mr. Kean chipped off a bit of the character here and there: but he did not pierce the solid substance, nor move the entire mass. Indeed, he did not go the right way about it. He was too violent at first, and too tame afterwards. He sunk from unmixed rage to mere dotage. Thus (to leave the general description and come to particulars) he made the well-known curse a piece of downright rant. He "tore it to tatters, to very rags," and made it, from beginning to end, an explosion of ungovernable physical rage, without solemnity, or elevation.

William Hazlitt in the *London Magazine*, June 1820, on Edmund Kean's performance as Lear in *King Lear*

❧

... the audience sits squirming in its seats, bored and embarrassed and uneasy, as though it had been impressed by some unhappy chance into the role of eavesdropper on a highly painful and intimate spectacle.

Mary McCarthy on Irwin Shaw's *Sons and Soldiers*, June 1943

❧

So devastating are the decorations that... John Gielgud's Lear is for some time neglected in favour of the Duke, who is wearing indiarubber water-bottles round his waist; the Knight, with a gumboot on one leg and a hockey-pad on the other; and the men draped with sausages.

Alan Bendle's review, in the *Manchester Evening News*, of a production of *King Lear*, November 1955.

❧

For here is stale and negligible refuse indeed. Here are the picked bones and the broken eggshells and the potato-parings of drama, embedded, with many other nameless scraps and shreds, in the dust of ages. But Nature is an idle vestry, and the opened lid in the area of the Garrick Theatre wafts to our nostrils the faint unwholesome savour of *Peril*. Here, I protest, is "The Drama of the Dustbin" indeed.

Max Beerbohm on *Peril*, by Sardou, 23 February 1901

He makes Macbeth ignoble, with perhaps a tendency towards Methodism.

G. H. Lewes on Charles Kean's performance as Macbeth, in *The Leader*, February 1853

I sometimes wish that the Trade Descriptions Act could be extended to deal with playwrights who fail to differentiate between play and monologue. Arnold Wesker's "two new plays"... are two forty-five-minute monologues for an actress.

Charles Osborne on Arnold Wesker's *Yarnsdale and Whatever Happened to Betty Lemon*. From *First Nights, Second Thoughts* (Bellew Publishing, 2001)

He delivers every line with a monotonous tenor bark as if addressing an audience of deaf Eskimos...It was P. G. Wodehouse who memorably said that the "Tomorrow and tomorrow and tomorrow" speech has got a lot of spin on it but, as delivered by Mr. O'Toole, it is hit for six like a full toss.

Michael Billington in the *Guardian*, on Peter O'Toole's 1980 performance

Mr. Quin, whose sole merit in tragedy was declamation, or brutal pride, was undescribably cumbersome in *Macbeth*; his face, which had no possible variation from its natural grace, except sternness and festivity, could not be expected to exhibit the acute sensations of this character; his figure was void of the essential spirit, and his voice far too monotonous for the transitions which so frequently occur; yet, wonderful to be told, he played it several years with considerable applause.

Francis Gentleman on James Quin

For the information of the worried, Quex is pronounced to rhyme with specks, or wrecks, or sex, as you will.

The New York Dramatic Mirror, November 1900, on *The Gay Lord Quex* (by Arthur Wing Pinero)

The scenery was beautiful but the actors got in front of it.

Alexander Woollcott

I begin positively to believe that (Shaw) may one day write a serious and even an artistic play, if he will only repress his irreverent whimsicality, try to clothe his character-conceptions in flesh and blood, and realise the difference between knowingness and knowledge.

William Archer in *The Theatrical World* of 1894, on *Arms and the Man* by George Bernard Shaw

There is a number of possible explanations for the presence of *Il Campiello* in the repertoire of the National Theatre at the Olivier. The one I like best is that it represents a complete and never to be repeated mental, physical and theatrical breakdown on the part of all concerned.

> **Sheridan Morley** reviewing *Il Campiello* by Carlo Goldoni in *Punch*, 10 November 1976. The play was performed at the official opening of the National Theatre by Her Majesty Queen Elizabeth in October, 1976

There is a total extinction of all taste: our authors are vulgar, gross, illiberal; the theatre swarms with wretched translations, and ballad operas, and we have nothing new but improving abuse.

> **Horace Walpole** on the ills of theatre

The sentimentality of Mr. Welles's acting, the nervelessness of his direction, the bare, mechanical competence of the majority of his supporting cast combine to act as a steam roller on Shaw's *Heartbreak House*. The density of the original structure is lost; the play is flattened out until it looks like a sketchy blueprint of itself. Mr. Welles's production can only serve to remind the public that the original still exists in the library.

> **Mary McCarthy**, June 1938

And now I really must go and lie down, and hope I shall feel better in the morning.

> **Bernard Levin** in the *Daily Express*, after seeing *The Amorous Prawn* by Anthony Kimmins, December 1959

What all this means, only Mr. Pinter knows, for as his characters speak in non-sequiturs, half-gibberish and lunatic ravings, they are unable to explain their actions, thoughts, or feelings. If the author can forget Becket, Ionesco, and Simpson he may do much better next time.

Review in the *Manchester Guardian* of
Harold Pinter's play *The Birthday Party*, May 1958

❦

That popular Stage-playes…are all sinfull, heathenish, lewde, ungodly Spectacles, and most pernicious Corruptions; condemned in all ages, as intolerable Mischiefes to Churches, to Republickes, to the manners, mindes, and soules of men. And that the Profession of Play-poets, of Stage-players; together with the penning, acting, and frequenting of Stage-playes, are unlawful, infamous, and misbeseeming Christians.

William Prynne

❦

If you were to ask me what *Uncle Vanya* is all about, I would say about as much as I can take.

Robert Garland, reviewing *Uncle Vanya*
by Chekhov in *Journal American*, 1946

❦

Before the end a feeling obtrudes that a bulldozer is being used where a trowel would have done.

Phillip Hope-Wallace in the *Guardian*,
reviewing *Inadmissable Evidence* by John Osborne,
September 1964

❦

To the Opera, and there saw *Romeo and Juliet*, the first time it was ever acted, but it is a play, of itself, the worst that ever I heard, and the worst acted that ever I saw these people do, and I am resolved to go no more to see the first time of acting.

Samuel Pepys in his diary, 1 March 1662

⚜

André Obey's *The Rape of Lucrèce* is a simple and effective little play... But no one who saw it when it was produced in America by Miss Katharine Cornell could possibly have suspected the fact.

George Jean Nathan

⚜

A strange, horrible business, but I suppose good enough for Shakespeare's day.

Queen Victoria passing comment on *King Lear*

⚜

Any American critic who has covered the European theatre for any length of time knows full well their nature before he starts packing his bags. He knows that the French stage is each season certain to disclose at least three or four farces in which various Fifis figure adulterously with various Gastons in invariant beds, the while various Fifis' various maids carry on with the various Gastons' various valets and the various Fifis' elderly spouses are eventually placated with the assurance that everything has been morally jake and that their deplorable suspicions have been born of evil dreams resulting from late langouste suppers with gay Folies Bergère dancers at the Boeuf Sur Le Toit.

George Jean Nathan

⚜

Once upon a time there was an actor called gruff Laurence Olivier, whose wife was an actress called pert Vivien Leigh, and a playwright called clever Terence Rattigan wrote a play for them called *The Sleeping Prince*, with a gruff part for him and a pert part for her, and to noboby's surprise it ran happily ever after, with twice-weekly matinées...

Among the select group of plays written for eminent husband-and-wife teams in coronation years, it ranks very high...

Kenneth Tynan in the *Daily Sketch*, November 1953

The plot is of such titanic and recondite imbecility that I couldn't reveal it if I wanted to...

Most of the dialogue consists of the members of the cast explaining the plot to one another, a service I can well imagine they need.

But I cannot see that they need the explanations to be couched in language of such shattering banality.

Bernard Levin in the *Daily Express* on
The Sound of Murder by William Fairchild, August 1959

... the play itself is like some stern piece of hardware in one of those dusty old-fashioned stores into which no Pyrex dish or herb shelf or French provincial earthenware had yet penetrated, which dealt in iron-colored enamel, galvanized tin, lengths of pipe and wrenches, staples, saws, and nails, and knew nothing more sophisticated than the double boiler. Ugly, durable, mysteriously utilitarian, this work gives the assurance that it has been manufactured by a reliable company; it is guaranteed to last two-and-a-half hours longer than any other play, with the exception of the uncut *Hamlet*.

Mary McCarthy on Eugene O'Neil's
The Iceman Cometh, December 1946

What a squib of play. Priestley's idea of man's revolt against stultifying environment is to put a coal scuttle on his head and crash about the living room in time to the Polovtsian Dances. Jesus!

Charles Osborne on J. B. Priestley's *Mr. Kettle and Mrs. Moon*.
From diary extract in *First Nights, Second Thoughts*
(Bellew Publishing, 2001)

～※◎※～

For Motherlant, history is dignified, and dignity is sententious; every speech comes tripping across the footlights with a ball and chain of pseudo-profundity attached to its ankle. The characters, so many robed machines for the production of densely scrambled platitude, exchange lectures on the state of their souls, the danger of love, […] and other topics calculated to exploit the full capacity of the French language for exquisite, lapidary emptiness.

Kenneth Tynan on Henry de Motherlant's play
Queen after Death, 1961

～※◎※～

I cannot, on my heart, take Sarah's Hamlet seriously. I cannot even imagine any one capable of more than a hollow pretence at taking it seriously. However, the truly great are apt, in matters concerning themselves, to lose that sense of fitness which is usually called sense of humour, and I did not notice that Sarah was once hindered in her performance by any irresistible desire to burst out laughing. Her solemnity was politely fostered by the Adelphi audience. From first to last no one smiled. If any one had so far relaxed himself as to smile, he would have been bound to laugh. One laugh in that dangerous atmosphere, and the whole structure of polite solemnity would have toppled down, burying beneath its ruins the national reputation for good manners. I, therefore, like every one else, kept an iron control upon the corners of my lips. It was not until I was half-way home and well out of earshot of the Adelphi, that I unsealed the accumulations of my merriment.

Max Beerbohm's review of Sarah Bernhardt's performance in the role of Hamlet, 17 June 1899

❧

Why is it that among the great artists of the world, whether male or female, we find so few blondes?

George Jean Nathan

❧

The Snow Man is not a pantomime to which all children, indiscriminately, should be taken by their parents. But all naughty children should be taken to it at once. It is, I know, a stern measure that I am advocating; one from which many parents will shrink, partly in fear of the S.P.C.C., partly from an incapacity to see why the sins of the children should be visited on themselves. Nevertheless, I advocate it. The sentimental way of treating children has been tried, and it has failed. Our piteous appeal to their better natures has been intercepted by their worse. It is well known that naughtiness is alarmingly on the increase. Parents must make a stand. Let them make their stand now, in the Lyceum Theatre…

The idea of an animated Snow Man who, with the best intentions, casts a chill upon all around him and freezes the heart of every one he touches, is not a bad symbolical idea for treatment in a book. But on the stage, where you see the actual process—and Mr. Sturgess lets you see it again and again—the Snow Man is quite intolerable. The auditorium seemed to be growing colder and colder. Our teeth chattered. We struggled into our greatcoats, and sat with upturned collars. Realism had been going too far. Mr. James Welch played the part of the Snow Man. I suspect he was as much depressed by it as were the rest of us. I had, however, no means of being sure; for he was hidden from head to foot in an impenetrable costume of sheep-skin, and had as little chance of displaying any kind of emotion as a sultana bound for the Bosphorus.

Max Beerbohm in an article entitled *Punitive Pantomime*, 30 December 1899

༄༅

Me no Leica.

Walter Kerr, reviewing *I Am a Camera* by Christopher Isherwood

༄༅

For all its frenzied breast-beating, this is a show with about as much heart as the Tin Man in *The Wizard of Oz*.

Charles Osborne on the West End musical *Miss Saigon*. From *First Nights, Second Thoughts* (Bellew Publishing, 2001)

༄༅

So-and-so played Hamlet last night at the Tabor Grand. He played till one o'clock.

Eugene Field's entire review of a particularly uninspiring performance of *Hamlet*

༄༅

Of Henry VIII, the American Repertory Theatre made it impossible to form a literary opinion, for between the text and the audience Miss Le Gallienne and Miss Margaret Webster, the co-sponsors of this project, laid down a barrage of dust: dirty costumes which seemed to have been bought complete from a theatrical warehouse flapped across the stage, wildly reciting lines.

Mary McCarthy, February 1947

Resignedly she bent over the book of photographs with the lover who had returned. Resignedly she lured him to drunkenness. Resignedly she committed his MS. to the flames. Resignation, as always, was the keynote of her performance. And here, as often elsewhere, it rang false.

However, it was not the only performance of Hedda Gabler. There was another, and, in some ways, a better. While Signora Duse walked through her part, the prompter threw himself into it with a will. A more raucous whisper I never heard than that which preceded the Signora's every sentence. It was like the continuous tearing of very thick silk. I think it worried every one in the theatre, except the Signora herself, who listened placidly to the prompter's every reading, and, as soon as he had finished, reproduced it in her own way. This process made the matinée a rather long one.

> **Max Beerbohm** on Eleonora Duse in *Hedda Gabler*,
> 10 October 1903

＊＊＊

One of the delusions about play reviewers is that they are fond of consulting with one another between the acts or at the conclusion of an evening as to the merits of the play they have been reviewing... Nothing could be more false. In the first place, the average reviewer is so enamoured of himself that he would not condescend to listen to the opinion of any other reviewer. And, in the second place, three-fourths of the plays the reviewers are called to pass upon are such utter junk that conferring on their quality would be as superfluous as holding conferences on the health of the stiffs in the morgue.

> **George Jean Nathan**

＊＊＊

The French authors evidently meant to satirize the methods of the police, and the result is a drama containing so much of farce that one cannot quite decide whether one is enjoying fish or fowl or good red herring.

Channing Pollock on *Arsene Lupin* (by Francis de Croiset and Maurice Leblanc) in *The Green Book Album*, November 1909

I saw *Hamlet Prince of Denmark*, played; but now the old plays begin to disgust this refined age, since his majesty has been so long abroad.

John Evelyn on William Shakespeare

This is not to deny that Mr. Sinclair is a good actor; it is simply to imply that his best part is that of Arthur Sinclair.

Stephen Williams, *Evening Standard*, December 1936

That Miss Cornell is a lady, I am only too willing to proclaim, if necessary, from the housetops, but that Miss Cornell is, in socio-political terminology, the first one of the theatre I fear I must gainsay.

George Jean Nathan, on Miss Katherine Cornell as "the first lady of the theatre"

Was there ever such stuff as great part of Shakspeare? Only one must not say so! But what think you?—What? Is there not sad stuff? What?—What?

King George III, quoted in the *Diary of Madame D'Arblay*, 1785

Days Without End...cries piteously for a poetry that is nowhere in it. Its lines are not only banal and humdrum, but—worse—at certain moments when only the high and thrilling beauty of the written English word might bring it a second's exaltation, the author descends to such gross argot as "Forgive me for butting in" and the like. The net final impression is of a crude religious tract liberally sprinkled with a lot of dated Henry Arthur Jones sex in an effort to give it a feel of theatrical life.

George Jean Nathan, on O'Neill's play *Days Without End*

Shakespeare's characters continually do and say what is not merely unnatural to them but quite unnecessary.

Leo Tolstoy on William Shakespeare

There was laughter at the back of the theatre, leading to the belief that someone was telling jokes back there.

George S. Kaufman on a "comedy" on Broadway

... the impression one gets is less of easy, unforced and naturalistic playing than of too few rehearsals.

George Jean Nathan on *The Joyous Season*
by Philip Barry, produced by Arthur Hopkins

The Case of Becky demands medical attention, and very little other. [...]

I was reminded of Richard Mansfield's ridiculous Mr. Hyde, who had only two front teeth, and that I used to wonder how Dr. Jekyll got the others back when he returned to his normal state. The whole exhibition at the Belasco, as I have said before, is as entertaining as sitting at a sick-bed, as dramatic as a surgical operation. You can have more fun in any good hospital.

Channing Pollock on *The Case of Becky* (by Edward Locke) in *The Green Book Magazine*, December 1912

❧

He maintains a gravelly, rasping note, hammering at you until—after two hours without an interval—you rush out thankfully to listen to the traffic.

John Barber in the *Daily Express*, March, 1951, on Stephen Murray's performance as Lear

❧

Perhaps it might even have been questioned if this play really were written by the G. Bernard Shaw we used to know, but for his unmistakable sign in the recommendation to critics, conspicuously printed on the New Amsterdam Theatre programmes—that before criticising Caesar and Cleopatra they shall read up "Manetho and the Egyptian Monuments, Herodotus, Diodorus, Strabo (Book 17), Plutarch, Pomponious Mela, Pliny, Tacitus, Appian of Alexandria, and perhaps Ammianus Marcellinus."

Henry Tyrell in *The Forum*, January 1907

❧

She ran the whole gamut of emotions from A to B.

Dorothy Parker on Katherine Hepburn's performances in *The Lake on Broadway*, 1933

❧

Whoever wrote the play's first two acts was simply a sloppy poet (e.g., his constant use of "the which" to pad out the pentameter), but...were he alive today, his scripts would be all over the wide screens. There is even, as they say, a picture in Pericles, assuming that the censor could be soothed. The fulcrum of the action—Pericles's flight from Antioch on discovering incest at court—would need what is known as a little fixing, and the brothel in Mytilene would automatically become a sort of wild teashop, but the rest is (almost literally) plain sailing. Before long the "working title" would be abandoned, and an item would appear in Variety: "De Mille rumoured dickering with Kirk Douglas for lead in upcoming blockbuster, *Around the Med. In Eighteen Years*".

> **Kenneth Tynan** on Shakespeare's play *Pericles*, 1958

Guido Nadzo was nadzo guido.

> **George S. Kaufman** (attrib.) on an aspiring young
> Italian actor with the unfortunate name of
> Guido Nadzo; the comment has also been attributed
> to Brooks Atkinson

One cannot picture the fate of England in India jeopardized by the calf-love of a youth and a maiden, and hanging upon the "yes" or "no" of so insipid a person as Elsie Leslie.

> **Channing Pollock** on *Disraeli* (by Louis N. Parker)
> in *The Green Book Album*, December 1911

Every year that *La Dame aux Camélias* is played it looks in some respects odder and more obsolete, and yet it is kept fresh, or rather in a kind of pickle, not really fresh but still fit for dramatic workmanship, in the narrower sense, of the younger Dumas.

C. E. Montague in *The Manchester Guardian*, 18 July 1898

The critics liked it; "nice people" will continue to go to it for six months or a year. Criticism could not deter them from it because its vice, an absolute vacuousness, is to them a virtue.

Mary McCarthy's review of *Brigadoon*, June 1947

There are three things to be said about Mr. Hampden's Shylock. It is squalid; it is aged; it is unbalanced and hysterical.

O. W. Firkins on Walter Hampden's performance in Shakespeare's *The Merchant of Venice*, published in the *Weekly Review* 1921

The play wears badly, partly because the serious lines sound solemn and partly because the comic lines are couched (as often in Shaw) almost exclusively in terms of rebuke—by which I mean the sort of brisk, hygienic, one-upmanship that nannies use to remind adults that their true home is the nursery. Very little about Candida interests me except the flagrant lie on which it is founded—namely, that Morell the "pig-headed parson" and Marchbanks the "wretched little nervous disease" are two different people. In fact, they represent different sides of the same person... Together, they add up to the exuberant, infertile figure of G.B.S.

Kenneth Tynan on *Candida* by George Bernard Shaw, 1960

"Of all plays else, I have avoided thee," I murmured as I took my seat at the Barbican Theatre for Adrian Noble's RSC production of Ibsen's *The Master Builder*. On my first encounter with it more than forty years ago, I thought It the great dramatist's most preposterous play, and its three leading characters too mad to be of interest. Recognising this to be a philistine view, I pusillanimously kept it to myself. […]

At the Barbican, I am afraid I found *The Master Builder* more than faintly risible. I appear not to have been alone in this, for several lines were greeted on the first night with inappropriate laughter. (The number of appropriate laughs to be derived from the play is, of course, strictly limited.) Although Ibsen's crudely applied metaphors and over-repetitive sexual imagery make *The Master Builder* extremely difficult to perform, I fear that the general directorial approach to this occasion has been singularly unhelpful.

> **Charles Osborne**, from *First Nights, Second Thoughts*
> (Bellew Publishing, 2001)

There are no human beings in *Major Barbara*; only animated points of view.

> **William Archer** on *Major Barbara* by George Bernard Shaw

---

Funny without being vulgar.

> **Sir Herbert Beerbohm Tree** of his own
> performance as Hamlet

I do not mean that Mr. Gielgud had no conception of Hamlet. He did, but it was muffled by his precious, strained, almost dandified manipulation of the baggage of the production. His own

231

performance was so decorated, so crammed with minutiae of gesture, pause, and movement that its general outline was imperceptible to the audience.

Mary McCarthy, February 1938

That which marred his acting, to the judicious, was that which marred his character—his colossal, animal selfishness.

William Winter discussing the American tragic actor Edwin Forest in *Wallet of Time*, 1913

Against this backdrop Mr. Weber comes across as a kind of yuppie Dr. Frankenstein, not exactly sympathy inducing. His glibness and carelessness of manner make his descent into remorse at the tragedy he visits on others seem less a function of selfless reckoning than of chicken-hearted panic and an eagerness to escape blame.

Bruce Weber on *Monster* (by Neal Bell) based on the novel *Frankenstein* by Mary Wollstonecraft, at the Classic Stage Company, East Village, New York, in *The New York Times*, January 2002

... it can only be said that Mr. Sartre's sense of sin is rudimentary. The crimes his characters confess to are so crude as to appear innocent and artless—a clergyman in the course of a five-minute solitary walk commits sins graver, more multifarious, more subtle, than are dreamed of in Mr. Sartre's philosophy.

Mary McCarthy's review of Sartre's *Huis Clos* (No Exit), February 1947

232

My dear chap! Good isn't the word!
> **Sir William Swenk Gilbert** speaking to an actor after
> he had given a poor performance (attrib.)

❧✦❧

The truth is that this is a noisily confusing show, and if a
few people sidled out on the first night, it was probably more
from bafflement than moral outrage...The result is a
strange, chaotic hybrid: a paella Western full of violent action and
constant undressing.
> **Michael Billington** on Calixto Bieito's production of *Barbaric*
> *Comedies* at the King's Theatre in Edinburgh, in the *Guardian,*
> 17 August 2000, in an article entitled "Barbaric liberties."

❧✦❧

House Beautiful is play lousy.
> **Dorothy Parker** in her review of a play called *House Beautiful.*

❧✦❧

There is an upstart crow, beautified with our feathers, that with
his Tyger's heart wrapt in a Players hide, supposes he is as well
able to bombast out a blanke verse as the best of you: and being
an absolute Johannes fac totum, is in his owne conceit the only
Shake-scene in a countrey.
> **Robert Greene** on William Shakespeare in his
> *Groats-worth of Wit*, September 1592

❧✦❧

Sapho, at the Adephi, is not a play to be admired very warmly by
any one who knows Daudet's book, or by any one who does not.
> **Max Beerbohm,** 24 May 1902

233

One should never take one's daughter to a theatre. Not only are plays immoral; the house itself is immoral.

Alexandre Dumas

❧❀❧

The play grated on me like the sustained whine of an ancient tramcar coming down a steep hill.

J. C. Trewin in *The London Illustrated News* on John Osborne's *Look Back in Anger*, May 1956

❧❀❧

The Clown (normally deleted, to nobody's grief) makes a brief appearance inexplicably hung about with tabors, cymbals, a recorder, and a syrinx, all of which he simultaneously plays, like a refugee from An Evening of Renaissance Rubbish. This zany interlude cleverly ruins Othello's next scene: one expects the Moor to enter with a banjo, singing spirituals. Shortly afterwards Cassio presents himself to Desdemona, astonishing clad in nothing but tights and shirt-tails:

Desdemona: How now, my good Cassio! What's the news with you?

Cassio: Madam, my former suit.

Desdemona: It's still at the cleaners.

Miss Corri doesn't actually utter that last line, though the situation cries out for it.

Kenneth Tynan on *Othello*, with Adrienne Corri, at the Old Vic, 1963

❧❀❧

Finney's roughneck Hamlet is no prince at all, let alone a sweet prince. More of a "Spamlet" really.

Jason Hillgate in *Theatre*, reviewing Albert Finney's performance at the Old Vic, 1975

Shakespeare, Madam, is obscene, and, thank God, we are sufficiently advanced to have found it out.

Frances Trollope

I have read the translation, a fluent effort by Bernard Frechtman, whose unseen collaborator, the Lord Chamberlain, has removed all the blatantly shocking words from what was expressly intended to be a blatantly shocking work.

Kenneth Tynan on *The Blacks*, by French writer
Jean Genet, 1961

The way [George] Bernard Shaw believes in himself is very refreshing in these atheistic days when so many people believe in no God at all.

Israel Zangwill

I am persuaded that Satan hath not a more speedy way and fitter school to work and teach his desire, to bring men and women into his share of concupiscence and filthy lusts of wicked whoredom, than those plays and theatres…

John Northbrooke on the theater

… an intellectual content which, measured in terms of alcoholic volume, hardly exceeds that of prohibition Anheuser-Busch.

George Jean Nathan, on the plays of John Howard Lawson

One of the greatest geniuses that ever existed, Shakespeare undoubtedly wanted taste.

Horace Walpole on William Shakespeare

It was one of those plays in which all the actors unfortunately enunciated very clearly.

Robert Benchley

The reason why Absurdist plays take place in No Man's Land with only two characters is primarily financial.

Arthur Adamov, at the Edinburgh Drama Conference, 1963

English plays,
Atrocious in content,
Absurd in form,
Objectionable in action,
Execrable English theatre!

Johann Wolfgang von Goethe

George Bernard Shaw, most poisonous of all the poisonous haters of England; despiser, distorter, and denier of the plain truths whereby men live; topsyturvey perverter of all human relationships; menace to ordered social thought and ordered social life; irresponsible braggart, blaring self-trumpeter; idol of opaque intellectuals and thwarted females; calculus of contrariwise; flippertygibbet pope of chaos; portent and epitome of this generation's moral and spiritual disorder.

Henry Arthur Jones on the Irish playwright George Bernard Shaw

Theatre director: a person engaged by the management to conceal the fact that the players cannot act.

James Agate, *Ego*

I suspect that Beckett is a confidence trick perpetrated on the twentieth century by a theatre-hating God. He remains the only playwright in my experience capable of making forty minutes seem like an eternity and the wrong kind of eternity at that.

Sheridan Morley on Samuel Beckett in *Punch*, 1973

Do you know how they are going to decide the Shakespeare-Bacon dispute? They are going to dig up Shakespeare and dig up Bacon; they are going to set their coffins side by side, and they are going to get Tree to recite Hamlet to them and the one who turns in his coffin will be the author of the play.

W. S. Gilbert, of Gilbert and Sullivan renown, on the actor Sir Herbert Beerbohm Tree

The German stage, as is sufficiently known, has been completely sterilized by the Hitler government; nothing produced there since the swastika superseded the democratic dill pickle has been worth critical notice. The new plays, written largely by Hitlerian press-agents, have been in the main either cut and dried valentines of love for Adolph or dramatized college yells whooping it up for the Nazi team.

George Jean Nathan

237

A fair example of "American style" productions is the Orson Welles *Moby Dick*, where there is only a tormented Caravaggist scene, of dangling ropes and shadows and sweat and staring eyes: toiling amateurism brought to a pitch of frenzy.

Mary McCarthy in *Sights and Spectacles* comparing English and American actors on a visit to London, July 1955

In the matter of soliloquies we cannot accept Hamlet as an unbiased authority. We merely find in him the possible origin of the belief that talking to oneself is a bad sign.

Max Beerbohm, 7 December 1901

A Taste of Honey is a boozed, exaggerated, late-night anecdote of a play which slithers unsteadily between truth and fantasy, between farce and tragedy, between aphrodisiac and emetic. [...] Twenty, ten, or even five years ago, before a senile society began to fawn upon the youth which is about to devour it, such a play would have remained written in green longhand in a school exercise book on top of the bedroom wardrobe.

Alan Brien on *A Taste of Honey* by Shelagh Delaney, in *The Spectator*, 6 June 1958

South Pacific may be a snooze, but at least it's not the dentist's drill that *The Royal Family* is... Peter Hall and his cast, led by Ms. Dench and Harriet Walter, seem to be under the impression that they're in the hyperkinetic, gangland Chicago of the newspaper comedy *The Front Page*.

Ben Brantley in *The New York Times*, 7 February 2002

For the theatre one needs long arms; it is better to have them too long than too short. An artiste with short arms can never, never make a fine gesture.

Sarah Bernhardt

Enticed by its title, I sample *Les Escargots Meurent Debout* (Snails Die on Their Feet), a long-running comedy smash at the Théâtre Fontaine. It turns out to be a one-gag show, parodying publicity techniques through the ages…The author and star is a plump extrovert named Francis Blanche, whose talent is the only attribute he possesses that could hardly be slimmer.

Kenneth Tynan, 1966

The Harringtons are a cannibal family in Suffolk. Snap-crackle-pop like the talking cereal, they spoon each other down reluctantly with cream and sugar at breakfast…In other words, they are a normal happy family—at least as incarnated on the stage by our modern young playwrights today.

Alan Brien on *Five Finger Exercise* by Peter Shaffer, in *The Spectator*, 25 July 1958

I understand your new play is full of single entendre.

Remark by George S. Kaufman (attrib.) to Howard Dietz, author of *Between the Devil*

I suppose it might prove marginally interesting to poker players but if your definition of a royal straight flush is the look of embarrassment on the face of Prince Andrew, then *The Gift…* is very definitely not for you.

Charles Osborne on Anthony Milner's *The Gift.*
From *First Nights, Second Thoughts* (Bellew Publishing, 2001)

⚜

The allusion to the parrot is apt, since Eliot's observations on human relationships in that initial, interminable act are one long string of cuckooed platitudes…

George Jean Nathan on T. S. Eliot's *The Cocktail Party*, 1950

⚜

*Carte Blanche…*the second of Kenneth Tynan's adventures in the skin trade, is a bitter disappointment not because it is actually worse than *Oh! Calcutta!* but because it is no better. […] Six years later, a team of seventeen writers, six composers and lyricists, two designers and innumerable others have laboured to produce nothing more than the same old tit for tat, with the result that *Carte Blanche*, too, resembles nothing so closely as amateur concert-party night in a nudist colony.

Sheridan Morley in *Punch*, October 1976

⚜

The Elder Statesman is a zombie play designed for the living dead.
Alan Brien on T. S. Eliot's play in *The Spectator*,
5 September 1958

⚜

The old words of dispraise—ham, hack—will not do for these performers. "Amateur" is wrong, for they are paid for what they do, and they lack, moreover, the one quality that makes amateur performances attractive: a certain zeal for acting, even if misguided…But these professionals are not only without talent, for the most part, but without the slightest desire to impersonate anyone or anything. They could not, one feels, get up a charade or play Santa Claus.

Mary McCarthy's review of a production of G. B. Shaw's
The Doctor's Dilemma, Spring 1955

※❀❀❀

I have always avoided setting up to be a judge of any player speaking a language of which I don't know enough to order a mutton chop…In consequence, I was never able to tell whether, when Duse came on waving her lovely hands and looking like the back of the kitchen grate, she was bewailing the coldness of the cold mutton at lunch or proposing to enter a nunnery!

James Agate on the Italian actress Eleanora Duse,
8 October 1935, in *Ego 2*

※❀❀❀

Curtain time is eight o'clock, and the whole plot is in the first thirty-six seconds. After that, the play goes rapidly downhill.

George S. Kaufman to the critic Herbert Bayard Swope,
to encourage him to arrive on time for the opening night
of one of his plays. In *George S. Kaufman and the
Algonquin Round Table* by Scott Meredith
(George Allen & Unwin, 1977)

※❀❀❀

It is hardly justifiable to class as a play a performance divided into ten parts, in two of which not a word is spoken, while the dialogue of the third might be written on the label of a medicine bottle.

Channing Pollock on *The Garden of Allah* (by Robert Hichens
and Mary Anderson) in *The Green Book Album*, January 1912

One of the most talkative and forgettable plays Shaw ever wrote…

Alexander Woollcott on *Getting Married* by
George Bernard Shaw in *The New York Times*,
12 November 1916

❧

The pitiful little thing has to do with horse racing, and you might perhaps say that it is by Imbecility out of Staggering Incompetence.

Bernard Levin in the *Daily Express* on
Dazzling Prospect by M. J. Farrell and John Perry, June 1961

❧

It requires a knowledge of, and interest in, and a speaking fondness for the English. It will be appreciated most by those who shake with laughter over every number of *Punch*.

Alexander Woollcott on *Too Many Husbands* by
Somerset Maugham in *The New York Times*, 9 October 1919

❧

The Birthday Party is like a vintage Hitchcock thriller which has been, in the immortal tear-stained words of Orson Welles, "edited by a cross-eyed studio janitor with a lawn-mower."

Alan Brien on Harold Pinter's play in *The Spectator*,
30 May 1958

❧

Synge is often praised for his mastery of cadence, and for the splendour of his dying falls. Dying they may well be, but they take an unconscionable time doing it. Synge seldom lets a simple, declarative sentence alone. To its tail there must be pinned some

such trailing tin can of verbiage as—to improvise an example—
'the way you'd be roaring and moiling in the lug of a Kilkenny
ditch, and she with a shift on her would destroy a man entirely,
I'm thinking, and him staring till the eyes would be lepping surely
from the holes in his head'. Nor can I bring myself to devote my
full attention to a play in which all the characters are numbskulls
—and quaint, pastoral numbskulls at that.

> **Kenneth Tynan** on *The Playboy of the Western World*
> by Synge, 1960

This babe may be highborn, but she is also born to lose…True,
when the legendary Rachel stormed through the part in Paris in
the 1800s, she was described as "an awful, ghastly apparition"
perched "on the verge of the grave." But Rachel's *Phèdre* would
probably come across as a strapping milkmaid if she had to stand
next to Kate Valk in the same role. It is unlikely, for example,
that Rachel's *Phèdre* required the simulated administering of
enemas onstage.

> **Ben Brantley** in *The New York Times*, 19 February, 2002,
> on a reinterpretation of Racine's *Phèdre* called
> *To You, the Birdie!* by the Wooster Group at
> St. Ann's Warehouse in Brooklyn

The only trouble with acting Shakespeare is the actors. It brings
out the worst that is in them. A desire to read aloud the soliloquy (you know the one I mean) is one of the first symptoms a
man has that he is going to be an actor. If ever I catch any of my
little boys going out behind the barn to recite this speech, I will
take them right away to a throat specialist and have their palates
removed. One failure is enough in a family.

And then, too, the stuff that Will wrote, while all right to sit
at home and read, does not lend itself to really snappy entertain-

ment on the modern stage. It takes just about the best actor in the world to make it sound like anything more than a declamation by the young lady representing the Blue and Gray on Memorial Day. I know that I run counter to many cultured minds in this matter, but I think that, if the truth were known, there are a whole lot more of us who twitch through two-thirds of a Shakespearean performance than the last census would lead one to believe. With a company consisting of one or two stars and the rest hams (which is a good liberal estimate) what can you expect? Even Shakespeare himself couldn't sit through it without reading the adverts on the programme.

> **Robert Benchley**, "Looking Shakespeare Over," in *The Benchley Roundup*, a selection by Nathaniel Benchley (Cassell, 1956)

She was so dramatic she stabbed the potatoes at dinner.

> **Sydney Smith** on the somewhat melodramatic actress Sarah Siddons

Antony and Cleopatra is an attempt at a serious drama. To say that there is plenty of bogus characterisation in it—Enobarbus, for instance—is merely to say that it is by Shakespeare.

> **George Bernard Shaw** on the play in the *Saturday Review*, May 1897

When the curtain goes up on William Saroyan's play called *The Beautiful People*, at the Lyceum, it discloses a set that might have been executed by Salvador Dali, needing, in fact, only a rubbery watch and a couple of lamb chops. This scene represents, or, more precisely, non-represents, the combined interior and exterior of a decaying house on Red Rock Hill in San Francisco. It is relent-lessly playful, rather pretty, and after a while I got awfully sick of looking at it. As far as I am concerned, this comment also applies to the play.

Wolcott Gibbs, *Season in the Sun & Other Pleasures*
(Random House, New York, 1946)

***

Having decided to focus on the hole rather than the doughnut, as it were, Ensler happily disappears up it.

Germaine Greer on *The Vagina Monolgues* by Eve Enlser,
in the *Daily Telegraph*, 1 March 2002

***

Two things should be cut—the second act and the child's throat.

Noël Coward on a tedious play with a particularly
annoying starlet

***

His performance of Othello…had not one good quality. False in conception, it was feeble in execution. He attempted to make the character natural, and made it vulgar…Fechter is unpleasantly familiar, paws Iago about like an over-demonstrative schoolboy; shakes hands on the slightest provocation; and bears himself like the hero of a French drama, but not like a hero of tragedy.

G. H. Lewes, On actors and the art of acting,
on Charles Fechter's performance

***

When Mr. Wilbur calls his play *Halfway to Hell* he underestimates the distance.

Brooks Atkinson

I've seen more excitement at the opening of an umbrella.

Earl Wison's verdict of a play

❦

There is certainly nothing good to say about the tragedy of Hamlet: it is a gross and barbarous play, the like of which would not be tolerated by the most miserable scum of France or Italy. Hamlet goes mad in the second act, and his mistress goes mad in the third; the prince kills the father of his mistress, in the pretence of killing a rat, and the heroine flings herself into the river. Her grave is dug on stage; the gravediggers trot out jokes suited to their kind, while holding skulls in their hands; Prince Hamlet responds to their abominable liberties by no less disgusting fits of madness. All the while, one of the actors conquers Poland. Hamlet, his mother, and his stepfather drink together on stage; there is singing at the table, a quarrel, an exchange of blows, they kill each other. All of which leads one to believe that this work is the fruit of the imagination of a drunken savage.

Voltaire on *Hamlet* by William Shakespeare,
in his preface to *Sémiramis*

❦

Tallulah Bankhead barged down the Nile last night as Cleopatra—and sank.

John Mason Brown

❦

Mr. Torn allows words to revolve wanly in his mouth like a jingling key chain in a bored man's pocket.

John Simon on Rip Torn's performance in *Daughter of Silence*,
Music Box, November 1961

I think they have made a slight mistake. They've left the show in Detroit, or wherever it was warming up, and brought in the publicity stills.

Walter Kerr on the musical *Ilya Darling*

I really enjoy only his stage directions…He uses the English language like a truncheon.

Max Beerbohm on George Bernard Shaw

You know I can't stand Shakespeare's plays, but yours are even worse.

Leo Tolstoy to Anton Chekhov after seeing *Uncle Vanya*

Ouch!

Alexander Woollcott's Broadway review of a show called *Wham!*

Who am I to tamper with a masterpiece?

Oscar Wilde (attrib.), refusing to make alterations to one of his own plays.

Was there in the play anything really good? Mr. Zangwill (if I am right in my diagnosis of the mood of a dramatist on the eve of a production) eagerly asked himself this question. He tried hard to find a reason for answering himself in the affirmative.

Max Beerbohm on *Merely Mary Ann* by Israel Zangwill, 24 September 1904

In *The Importance of Being Earnest*... the tedium is concentrated in the second act, where two young ladies are rude to each other over tea and cake, and two young gentlemen follow them being selfish about the muffins. The joke of gluttony and the joke of rudeness (which are really the same one, for heartlessness is the basic pleasantry) have been exhausted in the first act: nothing can be said by the muffin that has not already been said by the cucumber sandwich.

Mary McCarthy's review of Oscar Wilde's play, 1947

These Ibsen creatures are "neither men nor women, they are ghouls," vile, unlovable, unnatural, morbid monsters, and it were well indeed for society if all such went and drowned themselves at once.

The Gentlewoman on *Rosmersholm* by Ibsen, 1891

As Malvolio, his smile, when it came, reminds one of a crumpled tin tray after a lorry has ground over it.

J. C. Trewin reviewing Shakespeare's *Twelfth Night* in *The Lady*, 1953

Her manner of dealing with the delightful speeches of Portia, with all their play of irony, of wit, and temper, savours, to put it harshly, of the schoolgirlish…When Bassanio has chosen the casket which contains the key of her heart, she approaches him, and begins to pat and stroke him. This seems to us an appallingly false note. "Good heavens, she's touching him!" a person sitting next to us exclaimed—a person whose judgement in such matters is always unerring.

Henry James on Ellen Terry as Portia in
The Merchant of Venice, 1881 in *Scribner's Monthly*

❧

I have seen many curates on the stage. Indeed, without a comic curate a comedy is held to be hardly complete. Curates, from time immemorial, have been one of the national butts. It has always been felt that there is something absurd about them. And I fear that the instinct is a sound one.

Max Beerbohm on *Cousin Kate*, 4 July 1903

❧

If a director doesn't really want to do *The Shrew*, this is a pretty good way not to do it.

Stanley Kauffmann on Shakespeare's *The Taming of the Shrew*
as produced by the American Conservatory Theater,
December 1973

❧

This is one of the most celebrated of our author's performances; yet I know not whether it has not happened to him as to others, to be praised most, when praise is not most deserved…some parts are trifling, others shocking, and some improbable.

Samuel Johnson on *Richard III* by William Shakespeare

Admirers of the pallid and sinewless novels of Marguerite Duras might derive some pleasure from her new play, *Vera Baxter*, but I doubt it. Now being given its British première at the Gate, Notting Hill, it lasts only seventy-five minutes, though it seems at least twice as long.

Charles Osborne, from *First Nights, Second Thoughts*
(Bellew Publishing, 2001)

I confess myself utterly unable to appreciate that celebrated soliloquy in *Hamlet*, beginning "To be or not to be," or to tell whether it be good, bad, or indifferent, it has been so handled and pawed about by declamatory boys and men, and torn so inhumanly from its living place and principle of continuity in the play, till it has become to me a perfect dead number.

Charles Lamb, 1811

Her performance trundles on, firing on all pistons, like a combine harvester reaping an empty field.
Alan Drury on Dorothy Tutin in *Reflections* by John Peacock,
in the *Listener*, 1980

As swashbuckling Cyrano, Mr. Woodward's performance buckles more often than it swashes.

Kenneth Hurren on a 1970 performance of
Cyrano de Bergerac by Edmond de Rostand,
in the *Spectator*

Mrs. Campbell as an elderly siren was effective, but neither bewitchment nor singularity makes a great actress.

William Winter on Mrs. Patrick Campbell

The play opened at 8:40 sharp and closed at 10:40 dull.

Heywood Broun on a Broadway comedy

The most colossal thing about the average "big musical revue" is its stupidity. Stages with too much on them, and girls with too little, are supposed to atone for a plentiful lack of cleverness, with the result that the eye is glutted and the brain insulted. [...]

The Century Girl is intentionally bookless and unintentionally musicless—which is to say that, as yet, neither Mr. Herbert nor Irving Berlin has provided a genuine song-hit.

Channing Pollock in *The Green Book Magazine*, January 1917

...that glum three-decker.

Alexander Woollcott on *Mourning Becomes Electra* by Eugene O'Neill, 1931

If *Hamlet* had been written these days it would probably have been called The Strange Affair at Elsinore.

Sir James Barrie, quoted in Bartlett's *Unfamiliar Quotations* (1972)

Drag this tin Lizzie out of town.
> **A Washington** critic's comment on *The Solid Gold Cadillac*
> by George S. Kaufman and Howard Teichmann

⁂

I begin to grow testy with the new regime at Stratford. It has now given us a *Hamlet* as paltry and undercast as any I recall from the days before Sir Barry Jackson took over the theatre. In that unreformed era, when a dozen productions or more were rushed on to the stage every season, much expense was spared, and niceties of interpretation often went by the board; all the same, one could count on a certain basic professional assurance, which made up in heartiness what it lacked in subtlety. From this *Hamlet* even that is often missing. The production moves uneasily, as if mired in sloth and indecision, and seems no less tentative when it is trying to be conventional than on the few occasions when it ventures into originality.

> **Kenneth Tynan** on Shakespeare's play *Hamlet*, 1960

⁂

No.

> **Review** in a London newspaper of a show called
> *A Good Time*, which ran at the Duchess Theatre
> in the early 1900s.

Acknowledgments

The author wishes to thank the following for permission to reprint material included in this book:

PFD for quotes from *Ego* series and other theater reviews by James Agate, reproduced by permission of PFD on behalf of James Agate, © James Agate.

Alan Bennett for quote from *The Old Country II* and extract from review in *The London Review of Books* © Alan Bennett, reprinted by permission of PFD on behalf of Alan Bennett.

Sir Michael Levey on behalf of the Estate of Brigid Brophy for extract from a review by Brigid Brophy in *The London Review of Books.*

L. Pranger for quotes from *Thoughts in a Dry Season* by Gerald Brenan.

Rogers, Coleridge & White Ltd for extract from *Shaking a Leg*, copyright © The Estate of Angela Carter 1997. Reproduced by permission of the Estate of Angela Carter c/o Rogers, Coleridge & White Ltd., 20 Powis Mews, London W11 1JN.

SLATE.com for two extracts from pieces by David Edelstein, copyright © SLATE.com.

The Guardian and *Observer* for various quotes and article extracts, reproduced by permission of Guardian Newspapers Ltd, © The Guardian; extracts from *Guardian* reviews by Andrew Clements © Andrew Clements.

Mr. David Justman for extracts from *Good-books-bad-books.com.*

permission of Rogers, Coleridge & White Ltd., 20 Powis Mews, London WII IJN.

Punch for all reviews from *Punch*, reproduced with permission of Punch, Ltd.

Barney Hoskyns of *Rock's Backpages* for various extracts, reprinted by permission of Rock's Backpages, *www.rocksback-pages.com.*

The Society of Authors on behalf of the Bernard Shaw Estate for quotations by George Bernard Shaw.

Jeffrey Steingarten for extracts from *The Man Who Ate Everything*, copyright © 1997 by Jeffrey Steingarten. Illustration copyright © by Karin Kretschmann. Used by permission of Alfred A. Knopf, a division of Random House, Inc.

Roxana Tynan for extracts from reviews by Kenneth Tynan, reprinted in *Tynan Right & Left* (Longmans, 1967), reproduced by kind permission of Roxana and Matthew Tynan.

PFD for extracts from letters by Evelyn Waugh, reproduced from *The Letters of Evelyn Waugh*, edited by Mark Amory, by permission of PFD on behalf of the Estate of Laura Waugh.

Steven J. Willett for reviews from the web site Rant n Rave, *www.rantrave.com.*

Michael Winner for extracts from *Winner's Dinners* (Robson Books, 2000), copyright © Michael Winner.

Random House for extracts from *Season in the Sun and Other Pleasures* by Wolcott Gibbs, © 1946 by Wolcott Gibbs and renewed 1974 by Wolcott Gibbs, Jr. and Mrs. Janet Ward. Used by permission of Random House, Inc.

The Society of Authors as the Literary Representative of the Estate of Virginia Woolf for quotations by Virginia Woolf.

The Estate of Max Beerbohm for all quotations by Max Beerbohm.